Running On Air

by

Simon Hazlitt

**Grosvenor House
Publishing Limited**

The book cover picture is copyright to Inmagine Corp LLC

This book is published by
Grosvenor House Publishing Ltd
28-30 High Street, Guildford, Surrey, GU1 3HY.
www.grosvenorhousepublishing.co.uk

A CIP record for this book
is available from the British Library

ISBN 978-1-907211-69-0

Running On Air

Contents

Introduction

We live in a business world transfixed by the legacy of Henry Ford, where linear scale is everything. It is only by such means can you deliver a successful business by expanding margins and squeezing out opponents. Only by being big can you win kudos in the golf club bar. However, there never been such a tough environment for this "industrial" approach: competitors are only an internet click away, product life cycles are ever faster, markets change and fragment overnight. Products are fast being commoditised, the push for scale requires a bewildering turnover in staff, demand can evaporate on a banking panic and IT budgets rise inexorably as the amount it actually delivers seems to fall.

This book is about a number of things. Its first premise is that this old model of business is broken. The "Upstairs, Downstairs" structure of an MBA officer class (paid handsomely to strategise) and the sullen soldiery (paid a pittance to operate) has disaffected consumers, alienated employees and stigmatised business in the eyes of those they most need to inspire: our young people. They see the markers of business success as a paunch, a flinty disregard for their fellow man, and a Jag. They recoil. And it's not as if they have been successful businesses: long on promise, they have failed to deliver for employees, consumers or investors. Lacking any intuitive feel for the aspirations of its potential customers, all the business efforts are expended to squash any competition: customers may not like the experience, but they have no choice. The problem is that customers are becoming increasingly difficult to corral, choice is harder to squash and their scale struggles to deploy in time before demand shifts elsewhere (or disappears altogether). This book sets out to point to a different approach, one where a company's operations are more important than constant reconsiderations of its strategy, one where humans are employed as partners in the centre (not chattels on the edge) and where scale is swapped for agility in the pursuit of sustainable margins.

If you are the sort who has gone into business to be important, this is as far as you should go with this book. For you, the attractions of a good business will never trump those of a big one, especially with you at the helm. However, for those in it for the thrill of the entrepreneurial pursuit of excellence, this book might give you a few pointers, and (I hope) offer some inspiration. The pointers can be summarised as follows. First, to effect the changes, a business needs to appreciate that its most important resource (after its people) is *information*. Once that is clear, the book goes onto show you why you should separate it from the things it is often mistaken for: technology, departments, and documents. Once that has been digested, it's on to shooting down the next shibboleth: the management of your information by computer people. The Book enunciates a new approach which I call *Direct Computing*. What is it? In essence, it is business people managing their own information tools as it might its stationery.

Whilst no one would deny the importance of having pens and paper to express yourself, it would seem extraordinarily wasteful to employ a specific group of people to manage that supply, and commission an endless and costly series of projects to procure something special to fit your requirements. You just want *a pen*. Not only does a business save money on not having one whole department (and getting rid of the costly projects that go with it), they can do things much quicker: if you need a red pen, you go to the cupboard and get one, scribble a bit to get the ink going, and off you go.

On to the things which I hope might offer the budding entrepreneur some inspiration. This book is not about the formation of a radical new theory that might work sometime in the future: it chronicles the thoughts behind the setting up of the operational structures of Majedie Asset Management back in 2002. Almost all that I describe below has been done for real, tested and proven in some of the harshest environments imaginable: trying to find backers for an equities fund management business in a serious bear market, vying for custom against established global competitors and operating in one of the most unforgiving regulatory environments around, especially as markets crashed in 2008. After six years of evidence, the conclusion is irrefutable: the Direct Computing model works.

So, if it is so much better, why isn't everyone doing it? For one thing, this approach is only possible through the maturity of a number of enablers. The advent of cheap computers that don't go wrong too often (and cost so little they are almost disposable) allow for their use by normal people without techies hovering in the background. The ubiquity of fast connections between computers outside the walls of a company network offers the possibility of consuming technology from the best the world can offer (not just from those who wear your company's overalls) using modern technology applications that are "balanced" and independent, requiring no complex onsite resource to maintain and configure (you might have come across the phenomenon as "Cloud Computing"). These enablers have not been around for very long, so it is not surprising that we have not fully grasped the long-term consequences of them. Second, most businesses rely on their IT department for the formulation of their IT strategy, and the likelihood of them voting for their own redundancy is somewhere near zero.

So, am I proposing a risk-free route to guaranteed prosperity? Of course not. Like anything valuable, doing it right is hard. It relies on some talented people who are highly skilled in their business lives being able to make the right calls about their information management as well. It also relies on a profound change in the company's mindset to allow this to happen, not easy after years of project-based value destruction: it is about moving information management to the operating expenses line in the accounts, and away from capital expenditure. Such change is frightening, especially to those who seek refuge in process to escape having to be judged on the actual success or otherwise of their efforts. However, for every bureaucrat scared witless by this, there are many more budding entrepreneurs just itching to make a difference, for this book documents a new age where human skill is the critical determinant of *global* success, not some six-sigma process dogma preached by time-serving salary men hoping to crush others by scale. The end point? A business staffed with relatively few committed people with the tools, the confidence and the freedom to execute.

Part One

Beyond the Trifle

In your weaker moments, you despair at being able to compete on anything other than the price tag. But it's not all about that, is it? Otherwise we'd all be driving Kias and using Alcatel mobile phones. The truth, of course, is that we use a much more sophisticated set of buying criteria for most things than just price. In our modern self-indulgent world, we as consumers are looking to buy an experience, even if the underlying product is often something that can be shrink-wrapped. Take a pretty basic product (a print cartridge, say), supplying it dependably has a value that can be monitised: much as our economist friends would have us diving into the price-comparison sites every time we need such a product, the truth is that we are all much more likely to visit a site that we have used successfully before, so protecting margins and building barriers to entry for that dependable business. So all businesses are now, officially, service businesses: the key is not the product, but the experience; not the features of your product but the flavour you leave in your client's mouth that determines your success and your ability to stay as a bookmark on his browser bar.

And the most important of those flavours are familiarity, dependability and empathy: as customers, we all give a lot for the organisation whose touch points we know, whose undertakings are made informally and delivered on, and who seem to have our interests at heart. And the extraordinary thing is, in these supposedly super-competitive times, how unlikely we rate the chances of ever finding such a bunch, and how supine we have become in accepting the drivel that is served up to us by many modern day service businesses instead, especially the bigger ones. And why have we become so accepting, when we get so bolshie about other, more trivial things? Simply because we do not believe that it can be done any other way. The passionate, small start up that is driven to succeed is assumed to need to change as it grows, falling into the hands of financial owners whose lack of passion will be substituted by splashing out on "marketing the brand" rather as neglectful parents will indulge their latch-key kids' every material whim.

It is staggering how extensive this service failure is. As consumers, we steel ourselves before the telephone call to the insurance broker, the telecoms provider et al, paying out our hard-earned cash in a rush of relief, as that is the last "process" we have to endure on the phone. And it's not just in those service sectors that could be defined as "low value, high volume": my experience has been gained in the B2B financial services industry, where the same sense of disillusionment is felt by clients even when the fees they pay could extend to tens of thousands a year. What exactly lies at the heart of our disillusionment? It is the feeling of alienation, of being at the end of the chain rather than the heart of the business. It's the feeling of being lied to: "Your call is very important to us" yeah right. Only to take my money.

It is clear that something is very wrong with our service industry.

But, I hear you say, we've been here before: the traditional family business espoused all the values you've just been talking about, but were eschewed by customers in search of a lower price. Surely the dual targets of good value and high intimacy cannot be reconciled? Yes they can, and this little book aims to point you in the right direction. First, a little history....

Long, long ago, most substantial businesses were production concerns: they manufactured things with long life cycles and high localised barriers to entry. The keys to success were standardisation and as low a unit price of the widget as possible, achieved through volume. Innovation was kept away from the front line production environment, and customisation was minimal. As our developed economies evolved onto a more service footing, so "platform engineering" honed on the production line was deployed to support these new services. The "time and motion" men, so successful in the industrialisation of production, could now turn their attention to this new, highly profitable set of business activities. Except what was tangible (machinery) was now intangible (information), so they called themselves "Information

Technology", and set about transforming these new businesses using the trusty old metrics of standardisation and low unit cost of production. "Business Analysts" appeared throughout the firm's operations, tasked with finding out exactly what went on ("documenting requirements") and relaying what they found to the software factory, who would proceed to industrialise it. And how did they industrialise it? By introducing process. The aim was to build a system that was easy to operate and delivered the same outcome every time. Quality was uniformity, and being simple to use, the business could avoid being held to ransom by a few experienced staff (who would have been called craftsman in the previous age). Thus humans were expected to behave like machines, and the machines like humans: all the decisions would be taken by the "system", leaving the humans to process the consequences.

It was quite an achievement: software was, historically, a pig to develop. You needed large numbers of people to write the code from scratch every time, and building an environment where computing resources were connected to each other was tricky and expensive. However, at least once you did it, you had as tangible a set of barriers to entry as ever existed in the manufacturing world. Invest in the platform, and you could give yourself a competitive advantage. Senior business people, grateful recipients of this unique "production line", could grow volumes and widen margins in much the same way that their manufacturing ancestors did a generation before, reserving to themselves the huge rewards that would surely follow, unencumbered by the need to share them with any of their subordinates who operated the system, as they were expendable (and outsource-able). Perfect.

Except that it has never worked. Services are different from manufacturing: an enterprise focused on the production of a widget could allow itself the luxury of a little introversion, but services demand the opposite. And services, being the aspirations of your clients, have no physical form and so can change and vary infinitely. Mapping this to the expensive industrialised platforms attempting to support this environment was never going to work particularly successfully. Those Business Analysts did not so much analyse as translate: most experienced business people (if they had survived in the new environment), when asked about their processes in any particular set of circumstances, would say "it depends" - on any number of variables too complex to model. The Analyst, faced with these shades of grey, would "document" (simplify) them in a way that a programmer could code against, that of binary, or black and white. The result is that in relatively low value service sectors, reality has to conform to the limitations of the code: options are limited, and the customer experience is dreadful. The subtle orchestra of client demand has to be translated into the discordant chimes of the telephone menu ("press one for service, two for sales"). Thus Information was cleaved away from its sibling, Technology: the staggering complexity of a modern business, its many external touch points and internal dependencies, its potential to cluster in a form necessary to deliver on each of its customer's unique aspirations, its opportunities in new markets forming in the minds of its next set of customers, sit in a multi-dimensional space quite beyond the linear "left to right" process people. A company's virtual potential gets cramped by Technology into aspic, its profits sucked away by those same industrialisers who have so hobbled its maneuverability. Ironically, the measures designed to increase a business' linear scalability (how many of a certain type of product can it sell at the cheapest factory gate price), have destroyed its real potential to grow in other dimensions, by moving into a deeper (and less price-sensitive) relationship with its customers and their changing needs. To appreciate the truth in this statement, you only have to look at the lamentable record of that most beloved of business school concepts: cross-selling.

Cross-selling is a great concept. By using existing service channels for product A and inside knowledge of your customer, you could sell them product B: not only do you sell very efficiently, you have just made your company more indispensable to your customer, driving up pricing tolerances. So, the theory went, scale would beget scale, as the bigger you were, the easier it would be to sell something else to the customer, and so the bigger you would get and so on. The thing is, it didn't just not happen, things have actually gone in reverse for many industries, as customers have preferred to buy from a variety of smaller, more focused suppliers. Understanding the reasons for this breakdown can help illustrate how the modern service business has come up short, and specifically how industrialisation has failed to deliver its quoted (and expensive) promise of service growth.

Cross-selling, as we have seen, is predicated on the notion that information gleaned about a customer in selling them product A could be used by another part of the service organisation to sell them product B. For example, a fund management subsidiary of a large bank who looks after a company's pension scheme could use the access available to the company's senior management through the pension route to offer other financial products from different parts of the bank, maybe mergers & acquisitions advice, or balance sheet restructuring. In practice, this sort of thing is painfully rare. It wasn't that the company typically refused the well-briefed and clued up cross-sell either: most often one part of the bank would be oblivious to what was happening in any other, which meant that the cross-sell was never set up. Why? Well, firstly in the financial world there are very real regulatory constraints to the sharing of information across departmental boundaries, of course. However, there are enough examples of miserable cross-selling failure in other, non-regulated industries to see that the cause for the blockage must lie somewhere else. The first of these is culture: employees unwilling to share the details of their clients systematically across their organisations, afraid that to do so would destroy their bargaining power at bonus time. It's easy to be sniffy about such behaviour. Surely employees should, at all times, behave collegiately for the good of the firm and keeping market access details to themselves hardly falls into that category. Well, look at it from the employee's end in a firm where the top management typically take 90% of the spoils: hoarding in those circumstances is a rational reaction to looting further up the chain. (If you run an organisation that has this hoarding problem, look in the mirror to find the solution). Furthermore, the employee with the existing relationship may be unwilling to share information across the group for fear of what the cross-selling efforts might do for the quality of the existing relationship. In our example, the fund management company with a long-standing relationship with company management will not appreciate seeing a young buck from another part of the bank fly in for five minutes to go into hard-sell overdrive on a one-off product whose chief selling-point is the transforming effect that product would have on the bank's margins, something the company management would wise up to sooner or later. Don't expect to cobble businesses of different cultures together and hope to reap any synergies beyond the initial "slash and burn" type.

Last, there are plenty of well-run businesses with no regulatory hurdles, cultural synergies and staff who do what they are told who almost always fail to share information: how come? Call it the tyranny of the "process". As we have seen, the modern business is obsessed with linear scalability: the language of the modern service business betrays this, with talk of "lines of business" and "channels", conjuring up images of the past, with production lines, and rows of crops. And so, a little bit like a bowling ball caught in one of those irritating side channels, once a client falls into one process they will never jump into another one. Of course plenty of businesses have cottoned onto this, and have set up earnest cross selling working parties to get round the problem. Clients duly fished out of one process and held up for consideration for other channels by senior people whose last appraisal round was filled with appropriate exhortations: criteria are typically size ("global priority clients"). This does not work for a number of reasons: 1) such secondary bureaucratic lumberings by senior people are no remedy for the structural inflexibilities of the primary systems; and 2) their chosen quarry have as little idea about the other potential needs of their organisation as the service business has of its ability to satisfy them. It is indeed ironic that the means used to scale up a service business have proved so pivotal in destroying any advantages such a business might get from its scale.

And what compromises such businesses make with quality. Instead of playing to the customer's aspirations, industrialised service businesses have come to epitomise necessary evils that have to be endured at the lowest price for the least amount of time, rather like visiting an NHS waiting room, or standing in line with a bucket, waiting for a turn at the standpipe. And the analogy works, because at the heart of all three activities is the concept of rationing. The idea of limiting an individual's quota of water during times of supply shortage applies equally to the provision of industrialised service: the assumption is that the potential demand from clients would always exceed a service business' ability to satisfy it, so you need to prevent everyone asking at once (i.e. make them queue) and you need to limit their choices to those that can be answered with an industrialised process. Indeed, structural overdemand is positively encouraged as a queue of callers wastes your customers' time (for which you do not have to pay) and maximises your employees' (for which you do). Such businesses talk the language of empathy, but practise the art of enmity. Customers are not to be trusted to ask independently for anything, as the resultant myriad of different requests would be impossible to service in any scale. Thus a dialogue has been replaced by a system of closed questions that elicit one-word customer responses, ensuring that each one falls into a process.

However hard these service businesses tried to carve out efficiencies and improve returns, margins have remained stubbornly modest: faced with a sausage machine, customers pay only what they would for sausages, leaving frustrated owners to propose ever greater degrees of "efficiency" (inhumanity), further commoditising the service, undermining its value and dehumanising its workforce. Our modern business people have taken the potential goldmine of a service offer and crushed it into a form of manufacturing, where competition is on price alone. However, having pointed out the shortcomings in such businesses, I am under no illusions as to their attractiveness. For many, the sight of a hushed floor full of people and screens, all beavering away has a reassuring, impressive feel, especially if they are all your people. Secondly, these businesses and their clients can be treated like chattels by their financial owners and sold to the next buyer on vacuous promises of cross-selling opportunities before the dash for growth (achieved through "introductory" prices) has been rumbled.

It is universally accepted that the very best service is delivered by long-established, close-knit teams (or even individuals) in a low-volume environment dealing in an activity valuable and/or complex enough to merit human interaction. It is equally accepted that such excellence does not "scale" beyond the tiny enterprise, and different, more industrial approaches are required to take it to the next volume level. This book says such assumptions are tosh.

First, why the need for "scale" in the first place? it is still a given that it is a pre-requisite for the delivery of decent margins: we remain in the widget mindset that if we can produce enough "product" then all the little margins will add up to a big payoff for the few fortunate people who have installed themselves at the top of an organisation, paying their subordinates a pittance and trying to exploit the same economies of scale that their industrial fore-bears found. This is wrong. With a radically different technical and information architecture a modern busi-ness can deliver significant volume and quality *without* industrialisation, and without a Dickensian exploitation of the staff. Not only would a business scale better with the new tools, it would be a radically better business to be involved with for employees, customers and investors.

The crux of the new approach sounds beguilingly simple: companies should change the way that they deal with information, *and learn to separate it from the things it is manifested in.*

Every business has (or should have) an idea of the key drivers to its fortunes. Maybe it's the continued relevance and/or performance of its main product, or maybe the sustainability of a particular set of Government regula-tions (and so the company's market), or the value of its brand. From this analysis a professional company management team will often develop a set of "Key Performance Indicators" that guides that company's actions, particularly in the consideration of future busi-ness investment decisions. Complex accounting models are developed within this top-down orientation, and technology adopted to deliver greater efficiencies. Yet, the one area that is ignored is that of information itself, the core component of every assumption, plan, report, presentation that company will make. Now, most rational business people (and they pride themselves on their rational, analytical skills) will scoff at this. It is not ignored, but built into the aforementioned assumptions, plans etc. All very well, but information (as we explore below) itself is distinct from its representation in a report or its storage in a database, rather as energy is separate from a piece of coal.

So what? Information is your company's reality: it is the evidence of the bewilderingly complex interactions that take place between your employees, your products, your brand and the wider world on a daily basis. Relying on canned representations of information, businesses can be marooned by the changing reality on the ground, rather as the French General, who faced with growing evidence of the success of the German blitzkrieg in 1940, simply replaced the map symbols of his battalions to their original positions, as if such cartographical stubbornness could overwrite battlefield reality. And it's not only flexibility that a business can lose with the wrong focus, but some of the power of the original information, too. By "casting" information firmly in different departmental silos, patterns that could have emerged from a dispassionate analysis of the whole are lost as it is segmented according to organisational structure (and so the prejudices) of the business.

Let's now examine the reasons why businesses have failed to get to grips with information management, and mistake the pure stuff for the things it's contained in. Here are some good examples:

Departments. Since it's the Accounts department who produce the accounts, the two are one and the same. Wrong. One is a stream of data combining assumptions and lots of different numbers, the other the people who make the assumptions and contain mostly zeroes (not the last time I am rude about accountants).

Processes. The routine that goes into producing something is different from the virtual stuff it consumes and produces.

IT Applications. The databases and IT systems are separate in concept to what information they contain.

Documents. Yes, you've guessed it, documents are different in concept to what they contain.

Business is about getting on with it, not playing abstract games, I hear you say - but that's the point; we are all so quick to get cracking, we fail to distinguish the important stuff (information) from the solutions we have historically used to make the most it, at a time when the world is changing rapidly. This is perfectly understandable for many reasons apart from the ones that I have listed above. First, very few businesses are genuinely new, and so the present nearly always starts with the legacy from the past. This can have the effect of making you look at the business whose departmental legs exist to stabilise it in rough seas (rather like an oil rig), rather than truly what it is, an idea in the minds of its previous, present and future customers as to what it can do for them.

Second, the tangible is much easier for most people to consider than the intangible. The intellectual property bound up in a clever piece of physical engineering is easier for many to understand than that inherent in a financial derivative, even if the latter is simpler than the former.

Third, for many in our businesses, the desire to help improve the business is actually secondary to the need to move up a few notches within it. A thoughtful discussion on the information needs of the business will not give you bragging rights with your next door neighbour, and a fancy title on the business card: fighting hard to create an empire with you at the helm will. (You can always sniff these people out in an organisation; they complain about how many "direct reports" they have, going on to create intermediate management layers that only get ripped out at the next cyclical panic). Indeed, a measure of success is how far from the day-to-day operations you can get: British business is particularly afflicted with this, breeding a generation of overpaid number crunchers who look after the "company", which is strangely separate somehow from its "operations": In practice, touting the company around for that CV-enhancing deal, under-investing in its operations to flatter the "free cash flow yield" or whatever other clever ratio the City of London dreams up.

So, I've discussed how businesses typically overlook the essentially abstract concept of "information", favouring more tangible (but secondary and frozen) representations of it. So what?

A clue lies in the word "frozen". Our world is changing rapidly, and one of the most powerful axes of change is that which is moving what was *physical* into the *virtual*. Perhaps the most basic example of this is the substitution of the old throttle cable attached from the car accelerator to the engine with a wire that sends, not a pull, but a stream of digital information to the engine management system. Another is the "fly by wire" capability so touted on the early Airbus aircraft, replacing reams of hydraulic commands with those written in software code. The phenomenon has accelerated with the advent of the web, where physical transactions have been usurped by mouse clicks. Even the financial world is at it, creating "virtual" money far quicker than the physical stuff in the form of derivative contracts. Perhaps the most important of these developments is that of virtual human interaction in the form of "Second Life" and the rest: in the virtual world, possessions are practically worthless (there is no concept of scarcity value, as software code can be recreated limitlessly) and the cludgy drawbacks of physical time and space do not apply - you can get any "where" and do anything in the blink of an eye. It is world characterised by greater speed of change, a world where fewer and fewer bottlenecks exist: the "tollbooth capitalists" of today who currently charge for "access" (to the web, to mobile connectivity, to content) will find their expensive, fixed tollbooths increasingly bypassed by consumers roaring off around them under their own steam.

Now come back to the typical late twentieth century service business. With its structure firmly rooted in the physical, its turning circle is comically too wide for the twenty-first century virtual reality. By the time that firm is correctly oriented for a given product (feasibility studies conducted, project initiation documents completed, steering groups manned, requirements documented, timelines and deliverables for software agreed, functionality tested and users trained), the demand (or at least the valuable, price-insensitive sort) will have morphed somewhere else. Somehow a method needs to be found to deliver business-enhancing software into businesses that can live with the tempo of change only too apparent in the markets they serve, and at a cost that allows the modern service business a decent margin in the face of unprecedented price competition. And it starts by disintermediating all those who have traditionally got between a business and its information.

One of the most surprising obstacles is the Information Technology Department. After all, they exist to help, don't they?

I have spoken about the English habit of creating an artificial split between a company and its operations, but there is another split even more damaging: that between a company and the management of its information. It is so pervasive in business that we fail to understand how daft it really is: It is our best people who drive our businesses forward, those who understand the needs of our clients, and who are experienced and capable enough to deliver for them. However, we don't trust them to choose and use their own information tools, for that we have invented a separate department called IT. It's as if we do not trust our best people to write, and invent a separate department that may be great at writing, but have no idea of what they may be writing about.

Hold that analogy for a second, and think how awkward it would be if every time you wished to express yourself on paper you had to call on the services of an external agency. And, because that agency was a professional bunch, they would spend a large amount of time gleaning from you what it was you wished to say. Subsequently, a sophisticated plan would be promulgated with a timeline for the key deliverables, and finally some prose for user acceptance testing. The relevance, timeliness and fidelity of "your" eventual comments would now be limited in value, to say the least.

This is not an unfair analogy, as the ability to express oneself in software code is simply a modern extension of the ability to write: the business needs to understand how to deploy software code as well as it understands how to write, or do the accounts, for the reasons given above. There is as much value in being timely as there is in being accurate. It would also cost far less. What do I mean by "deploying software code" and why should I be encouraging good, upstanding business people to become geeks?

Much heat and light has been expended over the declining standards of the written word. Technology, it is said, is responsible for a "dumbing down" of standards, where excessive informality of tone and sloppiness of spelling and grammar has infected business life. The casual email tone is now the normal, even between organisations, and even that has now been superseded by a wave of yet more informality ushered in by the "txting" generation. So what? The written word is now but one means of communication for those lucky enough to live in the twenty-first century. For every monosyllabic text msg, there are Facebook entries: a cornucopia of different media, expressing in an instant what would take an age to transcribe: and all done by the individual, interacting directly with modern software. And what power to their elbow: as their lives, loves and experiences change, so they can represent that in a blinking of an eye in their virtual persona, with not a Business Analyst or project timeline in sight, and at very low cost. How strange the modern enterprise must feel to these people, with its cludgy bureaucracy and its strange "why use one click when nine will do" insular, grey, boxy software interfaces. What if your employees had the tools instantly to reflect the ever-changing virtual persona of the enterprise in the same way as they do with their lives? At a stroke the enterprise would be transformed from the physical to the virtual, able to live in the timescales of its target markets.

That's why we should learn to deploy software code. And, of course, in doing so, I'm not asking you to become a geek, quite the reverse. Rather than people becoming more IT literate, IT has actually become more people literate: the user interface has disintermediated the geek, in the same way as the synchromesh interceded to make car gear changes the stuff of normal people, not just petrol heads. And so we live in a period of extraordinary overhang, where the means to transform the information architecture of our businesses are blindingly obvious but bafflingly absent from the modern enterprise. Today's situation could be likened to the advent of the motor car, except in this case all employees would drive to work in motor cars, only to adopt a pony and trap in the office. The amazing thing is that so few people question it.

Why don't they? In a word, fear. Fear of the unknown and fear of the consequences of giving the initiative to the more junior, market-interfacing members of the business. First, the unknown: a proposal to abandon the channeled, industrialised and process-driven environment in favour of what looks suspiciously like a free-for-all is profoundly disturbing: how could key performance indicators be set and measured? How would we know what is going on at all times? How do we justify our management jobs? This panic at the prospect of losing control is not confined to senior management, either: the IT staff (to whom the senior business people look to for the provision of the IT strategy) are proud of what they see as their contribution to the business and are genuinely dumbfounded by the notion that their presence in an organisation is no longer needed. Of course, it will take more than a little book by me to change generations of corporate culture, for that is how entrenched it is.

Whilst the introduction of information technology thus far may have seemed revolutionary, its effect on traditional company structures and cultures has been tiny. Companies, as we have seen, have never really got over their infatuation with industrialisation, and its chief acolyte, Henry Ford: highly centralised, it is impossible to separate a company's information from its structure. Information on client needs is the preserve of the marketing department, the accounts the accounting department and so on. IT in this context is merely a colourful (and expensive) notepad: a personal tool that allows even the most illiterate to produce output recognised by others in the business. Think I'm lying? Just cast your eye over a typical first class rail carriage on a week day, and clock what applications business people are using on their laptops - not one instance of enterprise, shared software amongst them. They'll all be using personal tools like an email application, or a spreadsheet, things that they have at their fingertips at home. So what is wrong with that? Well, for starters they are using applications that don't need an expensive IT Department to support, wasting your company gazillions, and secondly the misuse of those personal applications is horribly destructive to your business, "bunkering" information into personal silos, the virtual equivalent of everybody toiling away in separate offices and never meeting to communicate.

Whilst there are shared systems deployed in most businesses, their cludgy interfaces and lack of portability depend on an old-fashioned human layer to translate in and out (something unlikely to trouble those paid to interlocute). The effect of this halfway house is to make existing processes vastly more expensive and little better than their paper-based predecessors. Thus the sole means of information discovery for any employee is to exchange messages with other employees - the dreaded email inbox. We all know what a pain this is, but few of us understand how misused and suboptimal the system is. To illustrate this, consider a scenario where you are standing in a field with trees all around you: take in the infinite shades of green, the movement induced by the wind, perhaps a stream and wildlife. Now consider the same spot with all your senses blocked except an ability to receive messages about the nature of your surroundings. It would be hard enough to describe a static scene, but nigh impossible for one that is dynamic: that's what a modern business is like.

So we have the worst of all worlds - a "modern" information infrastructure that consists of layer upon layer of legacy applications that are expensive to maintain and spurned by the business, instead preferring to deploy "cherries" of their own on the top - word processing documents, spreadsheets and voluminous email folders that at least have the capacity for flexibility and speed of deployment, even if they fail the co-operation test miserably and add nothing of lasting value to the business. How did we get to this dysfunctional, costly "Trifle"?

We are, as we say, where we are. But how come? I've been pretty harsh on the IT Department, because they have had a difficult task. Expensive and not fit for purpose - that's a pretty sad indictment of the best part of 30 years' hard work, but true. IT staff have been frustrated about the business' lack of ability to describe and anticipate their operations, and business staff upset about being asked to give up a chunk of hard-won profits for systems that seem to work against them, rather than the other way around. Was there any other way? I doubt it. Given the limitations of the industry, expensive, bespoke and inflexible systems were the inevitable result. And no one is denying the need for quality enterprise software: In these days of fierce regulatory scrutiny, it pays to protect, share and organise your company's data properly, not to mention the role good software can play in the coordination of your company's efforts on behalf of a grateful client where your competitors are only a website away.

Of course for many years the rudimentary, centralised IT structures deployed by the typical business were streets ahead of any tools possessed by the population at large. Scale really made a difference in the quest for information: to bastardise Marx, ownership of the means of discovery was in many ways the critical determinant of power. The early English state's ability to keep a list of taxable assets in the form of the Doomsday Book greatly improved its fiscal and therefore its military position, and the success of its Tudor dynasty was in large part due to the vibrancy of its civil service and the ruthless efficiency of its security services. The end of the Catholic Church's monopoly coincides with the invention of the printing press. The height of state control of the means of discovery came during the 1914-89 war, where monolithic superstates clashed with little thought of the needs of the individual: "total war", and the Nazi state's awful Final Solution were all made possible by the huge state bureaucracies that gave them a stranglehold on information. Such power allowed for the discovery and maximal exploitation of national resources and the encouragement of the "right" collective impulse among its citizens. It was not that there was not dissent: any study of the national debate in the lead up to war in 1914 in Britain reveals an impassioned argument surprising to those who believe they invented dissention during the second gulf war in the twenty-first century. But, lacking the tools to garner information independently of the Government and denied any means of coordination even remotely as effective as the Government, it floundered.

In that sense, the superstates on either side of the ideological divide during the twentieth century differed little one from the other: whilst western ideologues would like to drive clear blue water between the "free world" and those under Soviet dominion during the "Cold" phase of the war, the similarities were striking. Large-scale conscription, show trials and witch hunts, ownership of the "commanding heights of the economy" and a cavalier approach to individual rights were all features present in varying degrees and at varying times in all the major powers.

As the twentieth century wore on, the possession of the means of discovery widened to include large companies, typically those manufacturers inheriting the mass production techniques perfected during total war. As information management techniques improved, the means now existed to flex the levers of information hitherto solely the preserve of the large states. They allied the expanded productive capabilities with new-found marketing, selling and servicing tools that allowed them to grow to a scale thought previously impossible given the difficulties of command and control such distended structures would have presented in the "old world". Scale was possible now, the bigger the better, so as to beget still greater information advantage.

In all this, individuals simply stood in lines, either as subjects, soldiers, or consumers. A feature of this period was the emphasis on "duty", "loyalty" and "sacrifice". As consumers, companies marketed to them in peacetime as their Governments had exhorted them in wartime: purchases were an act of duty, the possession of certain totemic products an obligatory activity for those wishing to underline their "rank" (the company car was perhaps the greatest of these in the UK). Uniformity was, as they say, everywhere. And it was in this environment that many of our greatest living business leaders grew up, and has been etched in their souls. It is therefore not surprising that out of this has grown an organisational template that resembles a poor military unit, with its ranks and rigid command and control. In an era of limited information, it paid to keep people in tight groups, ready to deploy in a sales drive as others might have gone over the top on the Western Front.

So what has changed? Just as the technology of information management evolved sufficiently to allow companies the means of discovery hitherto the sole preserve of the state, so it has evolved further to embrace the individual. Now, not only is it a more level playing field for individuals in their interaction with companies, it's now downright unfair: equipped as they are with the same means of discovery as their larger brethren, individuals can run rings around them when it comes to exploiting what they have discovered. Scale, for so long the critical ingredient in the management of information, has become a millstone.

So, how do we square the circle? If it was impossible to avoid the wasteful muddle in the past, how have things changed to offer us new opportunities? And what steps do we need to task to make the best of the new opportunities?

The main opportunity, of course, is the internet. The advent of protocols for the connection of one computer to another without expensive hard-wiring, together with the development of a cheap way of rendering content (the browser and the various scripting languages) has, as Goldman Sachs has put it, resulted in a dramatic lowering of the cost of information. Ironically, these developments have been seen by business as a great threat: gone are the barriers to entry that big proprietary systems offer to large firms, and the access to information available to consumers has arbitraged away the large super-normal profits some businesses used to enjoy as quasi-monopolies. This is of course true. Equipped with simple, low cost technology deployable in minutes with little technological know-how, consumers can swarm, collaborate, and agitate at speeds completely beyond traditional businesses' ability to respond. Consumers' ability not only to search for information from around the world using search tools like Google but also rapidly access the knowledge of strangers on different continents using forums has completely overwhelmed the poor old employee, equipped only with their email inbox and an out-of-date telephone directory. This was not supposed to happen: how could legions of clever, motivated people spending lots of money on systems get so soundly beaten by Granny with a set of free tools?

Of course, the software that Granny uses is not really "free": it has been developed at vast expense, but offset by advertising revenue from those attracted by the huge markets it serves. And that gives us a clue as to secret of its power: scale (ironically), tons of it. In Part Two I will look at how to steal Granny's tools to compete more effectively.

Part Two

Direct Computing in Practice

In Part One we looked at how the modern business is fundamentally unsuited to the modern world: its emphasis on a rigid form, its dependence on hierarchy and its risk aversion. We got a feel for the reasons why we are where we are, through culture, history, and the vain frailties of human nature. What does not need my pointing out is how difficult such a business finds it to live with the timescales of the twenty-first century. With constant revolution, the business finds it impossible to settle for any length of time in one particular deployment before being wrenched off in a different direction by the next set of hot shot executives proud of their talent for "change management". The best employees are taken out of client circulation and are placed in internal roles, occupied with projects linked to the next great leap forward. A whole lexicon of business speak has mushroomed with it: dotted lines, flat structures, BPO etc. It is amazing that anything is actually done for the clients in this atmosphere.

Ironically, just as we put up with poor service because we believe that there is no alternative at a realistic price, we also display similar tolerance as employees. Surely such turmoil is inevitable in such a connected, modern world? No, actually it's not. It's completely unnecessary and a hindrance to operating in this new chaotic world. One of the themes of Part One (and blindingly obvious to anyone who cares to look) is the extent of the mismatch between the capabilities of the "outside world" and those of the modern business in the field of information management. Think of it in business terms: what would you define as a successful roll-out of a new system? 200 people up and running? How about MySpace's millions? How flatulently self-satisfied we have become inside business.

The conclusion from Part One was that businesses should divorce information from the structures used to manage it. But what do I mean exactly? When faced with change in the modern business environment, the typical business reaction is to focus on adapting its structure, as if the next corporate realignment will be *the one*, except it's the latency of a structure itself that is causing the problems in the first place. Without one, and the right people in place with the right tools, you have the speed to keep pace at a margin that is sustainable, even in today's cruel pricing environment. In the next section, I'll show how this can be achieved methodically, technically and culturally, finishing with a piece on how such a laboratory experiment can be adapted for the real worlds of legacies, egos and paranoia. And, before you bin this book as yet another self-interested promotion of the latest wheeze to sell consultancy services, what I am attempting to describe has already been done, and done well: Majedie Asset Management was founded in 2002, and now has an established position as a high quality provider of investment management services to some of the most familiar companies in the world with 19 staff, none of whom are IT, operating in one of the most regulated and technically demanding areas of business, that of running huge pension funds.

So, onto the practical. To build a quality, trusted service offering at a sensible price you need a number of things: first, you need an information system sufficiently malleable to cope with the volatility of today's markets, assembled at price that allows you some profit. Once that has been achieved (and that's some achievement), you can then sit down and rethink your approach to the people that run these new systems, empowering them to think like humans rather than treat them like chattels. Both steps require a fundamental change in the way our businesses are managed, nothing less than a change of culture.

It is surprising how dysfunctional a modern business can be. Do not think that everybody in the business has the same aim: it may be true that all the principals are united around the idea of growing it at sensible cost, but that will rarely stretch into the departments, for instance. Human nature being what it is, those junior souls who profit very little from any upside but who will cop it if something they are responsible for goes wrong will have as their principle aim to mitigate that risk, and who can blame them. Given that they are experts in a narrow field, their modus operandi is often impossible to subject to any independent board review, especially as they will be proficient at gently alluding to risks too complex for the amateurs at the top to understand if they were not to sign off on the latest round of gold plating. It happens at every layer of the modern business. Given our propensity to salami-slice our organisations into expert silos, no one individual can really weigh up and decide between the operational risks of say, running with an external provider of Customer Relationship Management software (will they keep the data secure?) and the financial risks of keeping an extra IT team on the payroll to do the same job internally, which will cost a multiple of the external solution when sales are forecast to weaken and the P&L to come under pressure. And it's not just the IT department that will behave in this way: who can gainsay the lawyers as they propose another set of legal acrobatics "just to be on the safe side", producing a set of company behaviours never envisaged by those who framed the original legislation?

This all tends to the conclusion that any business should be run along authoritarian lines by a single, all powerful individual owning every risk around: that is as undesirable as it impractical. However, encouraging those business people who are tasked with the central aim to think about the business at a level "underneath" those tasked with fulfilling individual competencies will allow the right questions to be asked. Modern business is complex, but it need not be as complex as it is.

How do we get there? A combination of a culture change for our senior business people and the deployment of a simple plan. First, the culture: down with accountants!

It is staggering how those we have entrusted to keep the score in a business (the accountants) have now monopolised the levers of scoring: To express it in sporting parlance, it is the same as believing those in the score box are superior to those talented at playing the game. Of course, there are many talented accountants who deserve their place in the sun, but that's beside the point: they are there because they are talented, not because they are intimate with GAAP. Is this just some sort of emotional revenge attack reflecting some historical failure to pass the exams? No, some of my best friends are accountants, it's just that a training in accountancy seems completely inimical to a feel for technology, which is what you need if you are going to effect the transformation I'm talking about. The reason? To an accountant, any spend in technology is bad, except where it mitigates risk. The result? Solutions to prevent the worst from happening, rather than enabling the best to occur. And, in a flash, it's obvious why the business is saddled with cludgy, grey box software: it's purchased with the account holder in mind, not the user. Even better (or worse) is the fact that it is "owned" by IT: a layer of people beneath the accountants who can take the blame if the projected benefits fail to materialise. The irony is, that the most talented accountants get out of the way when it comes to information architecture, as if it's done by the business (i.e. the people in charge of the business' *key processes* (see below), then the savings are eye-watering, the efficiency gains impressive. It's not that accountants shouldn't exist in the business, it's just that they should be left in charge of the accounts, which is all about keeping the score. Once that has been cleared up, the range of business skills in the boardroom should be widened to include those with a strategic grasp of technology and an understanding of information in general, and the information needs of that business in particular. This call is not new, and is manifested in calls for the Chief Information Officer to "get closer to the business". This is actually the wrong plan, as such people never really question the continued need for the IT department, as that's where they come from: in the same way as your father always thinks of you as a babe in arms, IT people can never really come to terms with the idea that the business might cope on its own with technology.

I've mentioned the damage done to a business' information innards by aiming the IT sale at those who hold the purse strings rather than those who might use the stuff, and that a different arrangement would save huge amounts of money producing something better. Let me explain. It's all down to the modern disease of confusing quality and value with *certainty*. To say "I don't know" in response to any business question (particularly where it relates to spending money) is the modern equivalent of saying "up the Romanovs" in post revolutionary Russia: you simply can't say that. So, a whole industry has developed to help out the floundering accountant as he (normally) presents the budget to the board: the industry of project management. Because the typical accountant will have little real understanding of the information needs of the business he keeps the accounts for, he will need some other way of demonstrating his grip on things. In comes the idea of deadlines, waypoints, critical paths as manna from heaven. What better way of making up for a lack of anything penetrating to say about the business they purport to run than to bang on about how closely they are monitoring the delivery date of a key new system? As a result, modern business people are prepared to spend five times as much as they need to ensure that they have a clear delivery date, and that the terms of reference for the proposed solution has been fleshed out, than if they simply know the aim of the effort, trust the people looking at it and will be told when it is fixed. Think about it. Under such a ratio, four out of five projects conceived under the terms of the latter arrangements can fail and still cost the same to the business as one done under the ghastly terms of the former.

Surely the former methodology can't cost five times that of the latter? And surely the latter is a recipe for chaos? First, the cost. The reason for the dramatic waste of money is not necessarily the aim of introducing some structure to the effort of solving a problem (a good idea), it is the unintended consequence of a project mindset, which is to produce a project *structure*. This is created separately from a business' operating structure, and imposes enormous extra cost. Employees are kept on the payroll simply as surge capacity to conduct "discretionary spend" when the business requires it (which never goes away, as these people, mostly IT, are very good at marketing their services to the business in the advent of the fallow period, and who in the business wants such an expensive resource to lie fallow?). In my experience, as projects swing into action, there are four times as many "project" staff involved with the project as there are employees from the business. So, does that make it four times as expensive? A bit more than that, because you don't actually file the cost of your business employees' time on the project, rather theirs go under ongoing operations. Let's follow that through further: because your experienced business people's time is not expensed under the auspices of solving a particular problem, it follows that their time thinking through a possible solution costs nothing. Get your project staff to do the same thing, and the costs will be considerable (the majority of the project cost, in actual fact) and the solution itself poorer, product as it is of Chinese whispers. *And*, because every passing minute for project people (whether internal or external) costs the project money, the calendar time a project takes from initial articulation to eventual solution is a proxy for its cost. This is not so for a business led project (you of course have the elapsed time of the developers, but that it typically of minuscule cost compared to the expense of the monitoring structure, put in place, ironically to monitor expense). So, there you have it, an evil deal has been struck: in return for a sizeable lump of projects that should rightfully flow to those that actually generated them, project people can provide the currency of management for those "leaders" whose only experience of their own business was the module that covered it on the MBA course.

Of course, most project people and accountants are not intentionally evil, and the need for the project superstructure arose out of a genuine (if misguided) desire to impose some order in the effort to solve problems facing a business. Surely the tearing away of such a structure (and the firing of the people within it) would lead to a damaging free-for-all, and/or a critical shortage of resources as the business tries to operate and conduct projects at the same time? No, actually. Good businesses (and the management structures within them) are all about the disciplined appliance of resources to achieve chosen goals. There is no more likelihood of a damaging free-for-all in the solving of its own information challenges as there is pursuing its sales effort (it just needs a little thought as to method, something I'll go into later). Second, if done correctly, a business-led effort to acquire information tools should take up no more of their time than they currently spend as "sponsors" in the grind that is the modern IT project.

So, we have the IT budget shrunk by at least 80%. Not a bad start, I suppose. But surely monkeys and peanuts spring to mind – you'll end up getting what you paid for? Quite the reverse, you'll be better off. I mentioned earlier that a solution created by a "project team" is likely to be structurally inferior to one the original business might have come up with. This, as I said, is due to "Chinese whispers" – the latency involved in the translation of the real world of the business into minds of those who do not know the business. It is then regurgitated back to the business ("we need to have sign off") in terms that the business does not recognise. All remaining effort on the project will be to ensure fidelity with this document, not to ensure that the underlying aim has been achieved. This is because the project people (and the accountants) never really understood the underlying aim properly, or it was never communicated clearly by the business. Second, monitoring effort by assessing the fulfilment of an aim is essentially a qualitative judgement, and is never going to cut the mustard in an era that needs data, KPIs, deadlines etc, and it comes back to a fairly fundamental question: is the *primary* function of management to allow its business to perform to its fullest potential, or is it to design ever more exhaustive tools of surveillance? Bizarrely, most modern managers wouldn't be able to tell the difference.

So, rather than let the guiding reference for the project be written by IT people trying to "lean forward" into understanding the business, let the problem be framed by business people "leaning back" into the information space. As we saw in Part One, understanding information is an oddly underestimated skill, but it's the one that will allow your business people to write excellent keystone documents against which a coder can code (or an information platform can be rented, more of that later). Ironically, with the project people got rid of, one of the prime reasons for the project superstructure disappears: the management of deadlines. As the project staff are extraneous to the business, it follows that their time is fully costed to the project and that the longer a project goes on, the greater the project will cost. Of course, there are other reasons why it might be sensible for a problem to be solved by a particular time (regulatory deadlines, a dependency for other efforts etc) but by far the biggest reason for trying to keep to deadlines is that it is a proxy for keeping within budget. With the business now taking over the job of directing things, just because they take a couple of months extra to crack the problem won't necessarily mean that the project will balloon in cost.

How to thrive on your own

For the purposes of the next part of the book, we look at a new business, existing for the moment only in the minds of its founders, determined to avoid the mistake of recreating a twentieth-century model for a twenty-first century reality. In other words, they have the courage to think, not merely remember. Their ambition is to build a service business in a global market with the agility to keep up with their customers and a cost base that could keep them competitive in this "flat" world. They have, rather rashly, taken Hazlitt at his word and included no provision for IT staff in the initial headcount, but have trusted in his much-vaunted two day course on the nature, structure and management of information to imbue them with the necessary tools to create their platform. I accept that a far more common situation is that of a legacy company seeking to change: I will deal with this in subsequent parts, but allowing full discussion of a "pure" model is a good way to illustrate the salient points of the new approach.

Before we observe them roar away and create the new platform, a word or two on what they learnt on the two-day course. The first day dealt with information itself, with the second dealing with the approach they should take in the building of the platform. First, the information. They went through a gentle rehash of the first part of the book, understanding how information is separate from the things it is typically manifested in: IT applications, documents, departments etc. But more than that, they learnt that information was sovereign, whilst its manifestations should be subservient: that is to say their business structure should flex around the needs of the information, not the information bent to fit the existing structure of the business. They learnt, in other words, that the business should cluster and swarm around the changing aspirations of its potential customers, not mangle those aspirations into shrivelled, shrink-wrapped "products" that are sold down "channels" that fit, quite conveniently, *their* present structure.

Second they learnt that, for this truly to work, they needed to think about the structure of their information needs differently from their thoughts on the structure of their business. The provision of information on "client" (name, address, etc) is separate in concept from the department that sent them the bill, from the team that conducted service visits, and from the team that invited them to a box at Ascot for a spot of corporate entertainment. Separate and singular: like anything that purports to be sovereign, you cannot have two of them. How many times do you see businesses with duplicate address records in their billing, service and marketing applications?

So, how should our entrepreneurs start thinking about the structure of their information needs? At the heart of the new approach to information management is the realisation that all businesses are basically the same: they do things for people at a price, and in doing those things they procure other things off other businesses, also at a price, with any luck below the level of the first price. Therefore if all businesses are basically the same, they should all have a similar information structure at their heart. Let's look at that structure in more detail. (I use the word *Datastore* to describe the different buckets of information as the word is not meant to refer to anything technical, like a database or an application. In practice, a Datastore will contain a mixture of databases, messages and applications).

The Relationship Datastore

First, you need the means to chart the relationships you have within your business, and those with the outside world. For many people, this looks like a CRM system, but it is much more: typically the CRM system is simply the means to ensure that you send your latest sales flyer to roughly the right people. Latterly, that limited application has expanded to include servicing existing clients. The Relationship Datastore as proposed here, however, is so much more. Not only does it allow you to log the contact details of your clients (and prospective clients), it exists to do the same for every touch point in and outside your business: your employees, suppliers, potential suppliers, client agents, partners, competitors. Logging the contact details is only the start, of course, as you want also to draw connections between all of them, and make sure you save the important interaction between them in terms of messaging, tasks and meetings. This is important, as you need knowledge of your "network" (in its loosest sense) both to survive independently of each employee (and so persist long after they are gone) and to offer insights more comprehensive than any individual could possess on their own. Notice that I have used the word "network" in a different way to that typically used by technologists. To them the term is used to describe a proprietary, closed system of linked computers that typically maps to a firm's physical build-ings, a bit like the electric mains. This bears little resem-blance to the real networks of business, the ones that exist across organisations to create value. By charting these in the Relationship Datastore you have taken the first vital step to creating a technology network that mirrors your "real" network (more on that later). In addition to providing a more comprehensive view on your "world" than more traditional, channel-based solutions, it allows for a much higher degree of service productivity. With information simultaneously available to many people inside (and maybe outside) the business, things that used to happen sequentially can now happen concurrently. Let's look at an example: In a service busi-ness, Fred has undertaken to answer a query raised by one of his clients as soon as he can. Whilst Fred is on holiday for a week, the client phones up to ask for the query to be answered. As Fred's holiday cover is able to look at all the email traffic on the subject which is saved to the account record and view all the client standing data (including notes to file) to understand their precise needs, he is able to pick up where Fred has left off, and deliver the answer to the client whilst Fred is still on holiday. Such a system levers open the closed, bilateral inbox and floats the relationship free into the group consciousness, rather than keeping it prey to the profes-sionalism (and presence) of any single employee. Of course there is nothing new here. Diligent employees will always share with colleagues any overhanging issues, and access to other people's inbox would yield similar results. However, such a system uses manual workarounds to compensate for two fundamental weaknesses of the modern business: they are nothing but a collection of individual knowledge silos, and that almost all information used by the business and its wider audience is denominated in messages. With a shared place that belongs to no single employee, the Relationship Datastore does more than provide a convenient place to store information: it becomes the reality for the company, a far more reliable version than that based on the perception of each individual employee. I touched on the shortcomings of our message-based technology in Part One, highlighting how unwieldy that can get in a volatile, changing environment. To be equipped with the latest version of reality, you need to have received and digested the latest email. Which is the latest email? The Relationship Datastore will get around that, providing a place to store the latest information on all your counterparties and what you are doing for them. You know it's the latest information, because you're looking at it.

For many people, the idea that the Relationship Datastore *is* the business is wrong. Surely the managers control the business, and they receive reports from the systems as to how their people are doing enacting their plans? Of course the business must have a crisp idea of what it is doing, and for that to happen a clear sense of direction must be enunciated by those in charge. However, whilst the management like to think that they have full influence within their firm for setting the agenda, this is manifestly not so outside, and any system worth its salt should keep pace with the changes happening in the fabric of the firm's relationship with the outside world, and be able to keep those inside the firm abreast of the shifts. In the traditional firm, its corporate perspectives come from reports prepared by middle management for those in charge. In turn, those middle managers depend on their staff for the information, often manually compiled. There are three big drawbacks to this approach. First, the answers contained in the reports will be heavily influenced by the questions asked: this is another way of saying the management will hear what they want to hear. Second, depending on your minions to provide data to show how well they are enacting the Great Plan is a recipe for delusion. We are all so sniffy about the much-reported mendacity of the Soviet republics when reporting to Moscow in the days of the command economy, and yet we accept the same structures in our modern business. Such abuse not only obscures the truth from those in charge, it also powers an enormous misuse of precious resources. It is unbelievably wasteful to have expensive people employed in large part simply to prepare such reports. The Relationship Datastore helps this situation on all fronts. Given that its reality is merely the unconscious sum of all that is happening between your business and the outside world, it is less prey to subjective/selective querying, less tainted with the understandably self-serving efforts of junior employees to present themselves in the best possible light, and allows those in the business to spend their time adding value rather than vying for the Booker prize with their latest fictional offering. Of course, there is much more to a comprehensive set of management information than simply querying the information contained within the Relationship Datastore: financial and operational information also needs to be added (as we will discuss below).

The Operational Datastore

Having discussed the rationale for a pile of information concerning the "who", we clearly need to gather information on the "what" – information relating to a business' core competency. This is almost always a requirement that businesses currently recognise, and that has been the historic focus of in house IT departments. There are, however, a couple of differences between what I am proposing and the traditional solutions.

First, it is important to stress what the Datastore *isn't*. It should not contain independent elements of what is primarily reflected in the other two Datastores, especially the Relationship Datastore. Thus data on the clients of a particular product should not be replicated in the Operations Datastore when they exist in primary and sovereign form in the Relationship Datastore, instead a *key reference* should be used, using a *key* that indicates a particular client and *references* the primary record held in the Relationship Datastore, together will all the rich standing data held in that Datastore on the nature of that client and their relationship with your firm (more on that later). Although this first point sounds rather trivial, it is vital and the biggest reason why firms' information systems are so flawed: by appending primary client data to various bits of the operation, a firm is in effect permanently condemning the client to be an appendage of the product. This is dangerous because it reinforces the temptation for companies to view the world solely from their own perspective, losing the ability to see things from the perspective of their clients. Another way of putting it is to say that such a firm cannot distinguish its information from the things it's manifested in, the subject of Part One of this book.

Second, even when firms might have understood the need to separate their information on their clients and counterparties from what they do for them, they make the mistake of overcomplicating the operational picture. Just as most firms are essentially same at the top level (they do stuff for people for a fee), so the essential nature of work carried out by different operational departments in the same firm is more similar than the departments themselves are often prepared to admit. To illustrate this, here is an example from my industry, investment management.

Most investment management houses will have more than one investment team, doing more than one thing. In our example, there are two teams, one running segregated portfolios of UK shares for UK pension fund clients, where those clients have investment consultants to advise them. The other runs pooled funds of Japanese Equities for Japanese private clients who use domestic brokers as agents. What a load of jargon. In reality, although they look to be very different businesses, they are really quite similar. To discover, apply the *type of* test. Let me explain. Both teams are running collections (type of: segregated portfolios/pooled funds) of securities (type of: UK shares/Japanese Equities) for end consumers (type of: UK pension clients/Japanese private clients) with interested third parties (type of: investment consultants/domestic brokers). Applying the *type of* test allows you to gain a clearer picture of what your firm does in totality, and is a crucial step in designing the skeletal layout of all your systems to garner real economies of scale, and to ensure it is as future-proof as possible. We will get back to the *type of* test later.

The Financial Datastore

Along with the Operational Datastore, the Financial Datastore will be a recognised concept in all businesses and putting some enterprise applications to work in this area is often the highest priority for companies. However they tend, like the Operational Datastore, to be a law unto themselves with costly duplication of core data like "client" and "product" whose sovereign manifestation lies elsewhere, leading to a separation of the "financial company" from the "real company". Second, they tend to be unnecessarily complicated, preventing anything of any sense to come out of them except through the manual intervention of specialist staff. This is wrong, as these systems should be the servants of the business, allowing all relevant employees to both get a good picture of the financial consequences of a given activity in a given time period, and also to use it to model different hypothetical scenarios.

The Reporting Layer

Once you have assembled the three Datastores to hold your information, you need to consider putting in a Reporting Layer over the top to allow your users the most flexible means to get at the broadest possible set of the firm's information. The critical thing here is to define your users by their need for your information, not who pays their salary. In the example of the investment management business, they have employees, clients and third parties. The *real* network for information related to the portfolio they are running is therefore triangular in nature, with three interested parties looking in on one set of data. However, most businesses have set up their *IT* networks in wilful repudiation of this fact, driving an enormous wedge between "internal" and "external" users of the systems. Most companies seek to compensate for this failure to empathise by splurging enormous sums of money on duplicate systems, one to report internally and one for external users.

Once you've cracked the definition of your users, it's on the flexible means of delivery for this information. It is important to stress that the information and the means to render it are very different things. Thus you should not lock any particular item of information to a single reporting channel; rather you should be in a position to show any subset of your information down a given channel, or any channels showing a given piece of information. Once you have clocked the need for content and display flexibility, it's onto the broadest possible set of your information. This is where *reference tagging* is so important. It's all very well making sure that as much as possible is available from your separate Datastores inside your Reporting Layer, but you'll be really singing when a piece of data from, say, the Relationship Datastore is understood relative to data from the Finance Datastore. Thus, in real terms, you can ally your client information with that client's revenue data. In practice it often means building bridges (or reference links) between (for example) the item "client" in the Relationship Datastore and "account" in Finance.

The core of such a reference structure should be, in all three systems, the client. The common mistake most systems make is to model on the current structure of the business (something I've gone on about ad nauseam). Thus departments will be at the centre of the structure, and their clients spinning around the edges. Not only does this give the lie to being client-centric, it opens the very distinct prospect of the same client appearing more than once in the system as a mere attribute of each department. We've all seen this in action as customers: turning up for two different outpatients appointments within days of each other rather than having them scheduled together on the same day, having two parcels delivered to you at different times on the same day by the same courier. It's rubbish service, simple to solve, but just needs a bit of imagination to step outside the structure of the firm and put the client first. By placing the client at the root of your reference data also has the effect of future-proofing your systems. Not only will you now be able more quickly to spot new trends in your target markets, you enable your own structures to change around the systems without large scale re-engineering.

The Practical Challenge

OK, enough of the theory. How does our intrepid bunch of entrepreneurs go about actually building their systems from scratch, with not an internal IT person in sight and only a few days tutelage from Hazlitt? This can all seem very daunting, as these things seem very complicated.

Actually it needn't be. In fact, the fact that existing systems are so complicated is one of the main reasons why they fail (too little *type of* analysis undertaken). Before they get completely overwhelmed by the prospect, it's worth taking a few minutes to go over where they *do* know about information systems; those they have at home. Almost everybody has at least one computer at home these days, and many have more than one. And whilst most people would not claim to be fully qualified network engineers, they have managed to get the computers talking to each other. More than that, they've managed to hook up with Granny in Australia and Uncle Bert in Sheffield, happily sharing information and, if under 30, collaborating through networking sites, a step further than just messaging. In the home they might have a wireless hub, and it's now a pretty straightforward task to plug that in to the telephone socket, turn it on and go through the configuration wizard to set it up. Linking the house's computers to that hub is equally straightforward, and if they are really showing off they've managed to get one computer to "host" the printing activities for all the other ones in the house.

Even if that is the extent of the direct networking between the computers achieved, that's all you need, because all the other links happen via servers on the internet. So they might access your email from Applemail on a Mac in the living room, but they can also access the same inbox by logging into their email provider's website from their pc in the study or from the mobile phone as they dash to their pilates class, with the same list of contacts that sits on all three devices. Perhaps Uncle Bert has a cottage in France, and he needs a simple way to let everyone know when it is free for other members of the family to use. What could be easier than to set up a free online calendar, allowing everyone to see where the gaps are and to place bookings that others can see in real time? Of course it takes a few minutes to set up, but is less fiddly than sorting out the new flat screen telly.

And there you have it. They actually know far more than they think, because the technology enablers for the modern enterprise are actually far more visible to us as consumers as they are to us as employees. Many people will take exception to this. Surely I am not suggesting that "business critical" processes can run on the equivalent of Uncle Bert's PC with some free software? No, of course not, but I'm simply making the point that we participate in very sophisticated information transactions as a matter of course at home using simple, robust technology. Not only should that *architecture* be adopted in the enterprise, but also those in the business are more qualified to manage it than they think.

So what is this "architecture"? It is a combination of simple computers (the sort you might pick up from PC World or Target) linked to external, specialised providers of business systems accessible over the internet either through the simple browser, or through a piece of software downloaded to the PC (like Microsoft Outlook, configured to get email from a server over the internet). The critical difference here between this architecture and the twentieth century version in use in most enterprises is that, at home, the computers point outwards for their information: in the enterprise, they point inwards. So what? Well, the superiority of the outwards-pointing model is obvious when you clock even the lowliest employee checking their email and networking profile at lunchtime (if they are allowed to by the Dickensian dictators that still run many businesses). They do so for *free,* happily indulging in an activity high in cost and way beyond in capability what most businesses can do (that is: connecting to valuable people outside the firm in a collaborative way anywhere you can find an internet connection).

Hang on, I hear you say, I can hear the howls of outrage from here. What about the security issues and the empty feeling in the bottom of the stomach when contemplating the loss of control when abdicating control of your applications? This is a crucial issue, one that is almost always raised when the subject of "cloud (Uncle Bert) computing" is raised. So, first the security.

There is nothing inherently inferior about third party applications from a security perspective. Assuming that you have taken sensible precautions to cover your tracks when communicating with them over the internet (using secure sockets layer encryption, aka http*s*), there is no technical reason why a company hosting your application in California (where many of them seem to be) is more likely to suffer an intrusion than the bunch who host your own applications in-house. It is an internal IT fallacy to say that the business trusts their own IT staff to safeguard their data better than a third party. To the business, they're all slightly weird people wearing Homer Simpson ties. The only difference with internal staff is that they charge 100% of their salary and bonus to the business, rather than a fraction if working for a third party. However, that's not to say that either architecture offers complete security: for the business, it comes down to who cares more about trying to keep it secure.

On that score, the first thought might be that the internal crew must care more; after all, they are on the payroll, and so feel more aligned to the business than some dispassionate third party. Are you sure? If experience as reported is correct, most information theft comes from inside an IT organisation. In the case of the internal department, a theft by a temp who is summarily dismissed incurs little in the way of opprobrium for the senior internal IT managers: in the case of the third party, such a theft would most likely lead to a loss of revenue, and so pay check. Who's going to care more? With this in mind, concentration will be sharpest at the third party on information security, as they understand the ramifications: not only the loss of revenue from the injured party, but also from others concerned at the reputational erosion. Loss of data = loss of business. You cannot say the same thing about your internal IT department. There are further advantages for the third party IT provider when it comes to security: applications designed for web delivery will (in the case of good third party providers) be *hardened* with this in mind. Because they know their front door leads onto the high street, much care and attention is paid to the locks. In the case of the internal application, it sits internally on a network where the temptation is to rely on the network firewall to keep intruders out. Once you're in, you're quids in. When it comes to application availability (another big issue for enterprise types), the same issues of motivation apply: to lose the internal operations system for half a day may prompt internal annoyance (and a stream of defensive jargon from the IT department). Lose it from an external provider and the third party supplier could (if the business has done its procurement right, more on that later) be looking down the barrel of a contract loss. I know who's going to be concentrating more on the basics.

So what about that empty feeling in the stomach at the loss of control?

The truth is that the business has sublet its control of information to third parties for the best part of the last half century: giving that control over to external agencies merely represents a much more efficient way of doing it. In truth this is another IT fallacy, where they fail to understand how their own business views them in the first place. A good analogy is with the electricity industry at the turn of the last century. At that time, many big firms had their own electricity generating capacity (and, in the case of some businesses, their own board director for Electricity). It involved the employment of many highly specialised (and expensive) staff to generate a firm-wide grid, often at bespoke voltages. Contrast that with our attitude today to electricity, where we are happy to consume it in standard specifications from faceless third parties, even whilst we acknowledge how important it is for us (indeed, the grid in inherently less robust than the internet, itself designed specifically to survive a nuclear war). Would we prefer to consume IT from people we recognise in the canteen? Maybe, but we understand how much more expensive it would be, and we recognise it is not the presence of electricity within a business itself, but what we do with it that is the determinant of value. The same is true of technology.

So much for security and control. It's different, but you'll get over it. But what about the *quality* of the architecture I'm proposing? The first advantage is that of cost. Having no IT staff around and eschewing the project way of doing things will dramatically lower the cost of securing information services for both internal and external consumers. There is quite a bit of disagreement about this point among the pundits: they point to the fact that the per seat rental model of the external supplier really racks up the cost of an application in a business compared to one the internal IT staff can provide locally on the network. This is rather missing the point. The external service provided alongside internal ones is the worst of all worlds. You have still got the IT empire to pay for in this model, and using the external provider for an individual application will not change or reduce their load (and therefore their cost). It is indeed often cheaper to let those same IT staff provide the application than an external provider (except that it is a massive retrograde step, as we will discuss later). Second, "externalising" your architecture is about more than just picking a supplier for one of your line of business applications: it is about the fundamental separation of your business structure from your information systems. To plonk a web-delivered application into an unreconstructed business is like putting airline fuel into a lawnmower, it's much more expensive, and yields no greater performance. Make no mistake about it: going the whole hog and completely "externalising" your information systems will save you a bundle of money.

So, cheap and cheerful? Far from it. Here's some of the reasons to go "external".

1. Making your systems independent of your business structure will offer greater survivability (the systems don't have to change every time you get a hot shot MBA with a transformation plan) and manoeuverability (being virtual and inherently more flexible) your systems can move at "swarm speed", like your twenty-first century markets.

2. Your systems (and the information they contain) will be available for your employees and clients everywhere at no extra cost, transforming your internal efficiency, flexibility and external relationships.

3. It allows you to construct your systems around the *real* network, not the artificial one which drives a wedge (called a firewall) between your business and your clients, ridiculously discriminating on the basis of company allegiance.

4. Externalised systems are vastly more resilient in the event of a localised failure of power, denial of office use or almost any other Business Continuity scenario. The internet itself was built to withstand the detonation of a nuke in the atmosphere, so its benefits of scale, redundancy (in the sense that there is no one way through the maze of routers and servers that make up the internet) and geographic spread make it the ideal way to distribute your information. No longer do you need to think about your "alternate location": the world is your alternate location.

5. Externalised systems can be your business' ally in famine and feast. As a start up, its rental model takes immense pressure of the profit and loss account which might otherwise have to bear the brunt of outright systems purchase and (kerrrching!) the fees of systems and integration consultants. You can have the same capabilities as the big boys, but the turning circle of a gnat. As the business grows, so do your data volumes. With no physical limits, your virtual system can scale to accommodate a "feast", ensuring that your expansion is not accompanied by a loss of quality. In "famine", the system can shrink a lot less painfully than a growth strategy that involved a bloating the payroll.

6. Because successful external providers of IT applications have had to consider a myriad of different types of business when building their app, the best of the external systems are actually more flexible than those built in house, usually using highly specialised requirements. This turns orthodoxy on its head, where the main criticism of web apps has been their lack of customisation. Of course, external apps do not fit well in with the traditional "requirements gathering" approach to IT projects. However, the main problem here is not the external applications' ability to respond to the traditional process, but that the traditional process itself is wrong. As I mentioned earlier, all businesses are basically the same, and the differences in approach to common problems in a business have evolved as a result of the personalities in the business and the tools available to it to do the work at the time. All the "requirements gathering"

exercise does is freeze the current process and attempt to fashion the new tools to conform to it (a bit like trying to re-engineer the interior of a car to accommodate a bespoke equestrian saddle), rather than looking at the underlying problem in conjunction with the new tools and let the solution fall out.

Not only will the best of the external systems allow for more options at the inception stage, they offer far greater flexibility once the business has started to use it. This is because the external application designers have done all the hard work upfront, designing a system that can be used in many different ways. This is a logical effort for them, as to do so guarantees the widest possible audience, important in their volume game. So, as a business changes it can alter the way it uses the same external application, dramatically improving its turning circle at a vastly reduced cost and risk.

7. Working with external applications also avoids the "theoretic" risk endemic in so many internal IT projects. Significant costs are typically racked up in any traditional project before anything tangible is actually produced to show for all the money and business time expended. This is a bit like handing over the ransom money without securing the release of the hostage. Thus, in theory, the software will be delivered to the client on time, on budget and meeting the requirements as laid out (and amended) during the life of the project. Yeah, right. It never happens, so this is less a risk than a certainty of disappointment. With an external application, the business

simply gets to grips with the tool and learns how to use it to achieve their goals from day one, with no room for the technologists to promise that, in theory, their tool will be ready in time. If it doesn't work now, find another one that does. The minimum of time and money wasted.

8. Because the external app is typically (although not always) delivered through the browser on the end user PC, the training bill to use the system will not be large, as the best of the apps follow the conventions on web applications used by the big popular sites like Google, eBay, Yahoo and the like. Rolling something out becomes as simple as putting a URL as a link in an email with maybe a PC movie file detailing how people should use it.

So, vastly cheaper and immeasurably better, the architectural answer lies in the bespoke assembly of a series of external applications into a virtual information platform that is scalable, malleable, high quality and a real differentiator for your business. Easy really. Let's now go into the nitty gritty of how to do it.

The first thing our start up needs to do is a *Virtual Audit*. In order to drive the rest of the thinking, someone needs to conduct a thorough survey of the firm's market, and the needs of the firm in fulfilling them. So what, I hear you say: that's the Marketing Director and COO do every year. However, this one is a little bit different, and more basic. In particular, the Virtual Audit covers the following subjects:

What are the key information inputs for the business?

What are the key processes that occur within the business?

What are the main outputs for the business?

What are the main constituencies for that output?

Pretty simple, I'm sure you'd agree. But sometimes the simple questions are the hardest to ask. Let's look at each of them in some detail.

Information Inputs

First, let's define what I mean by an "input". An input, for the purposes of the Virtual Audit, is something that forms the basis of one or more of the firm's core processes.

The most obvious things that spring to mind are information feeds (the sort of thing that investment managers need: stock prices, research etc) but my definition also encompasses "standing data", the stuff that the processes need in order to function correctly. Examples include client contact details in the form of "address", "email address" etc. More subtle and less structured examples include client opinion, bespoke client requirements, competitor feedback etc. Where does "input" stop, and "key process" start? Good question. It would vary from firm to firm, but one failsafe way to tell is to ask yourself the question of who "owns" a particular piece of information. If it is an external party (like a client address), then it is an input. If you own it, for instance the price of a particular product, then it is part of your key processes. A more pertinent question I hear you asking is why do such semantics actually matter?

It matters because the exercise will tease out where your value really lies in the eyes of the client, and where it does not. For instance, in my world of investment management, a fund manager's value lies in running a portfolio that outperforms its benchmark and being able to explain its actions cogently and succinctly to its clients. It does not lie in the accurate pricing of securities, the collection of income on those securities, or (in the vast majority of cases) the in house development of complex technology. It's not that these things are unimportant, far from it: but they are best done by somebody else (sometimes, of course, the client), and the firm's responsibility lies in the efficient collection and maintenance of such inputs *independent of the key processes that might use them at any particular time.*

Processes

So, let's now look at the firm's key processes, or put it another way, the things the firm does that creates its value. It's important at this stage not to be seduced by the siren claims of the vendors whose trick is to persuade you that the shape of your problem is the shape of their solution (and nobody else's). Step away from the proposed solutions, and look at the problems. A help at this stage is to think of that architecture of the Datastores I introduced earlier: consider your problems in the three buckets of Relationships, Operations, and Finance. Why is this? It's all to do with that thorny issue that bedevils IT, the issue of *integration.*

The need to integrate everything to each other is often a favourite topic of conversation for internal IT staff when rejecting the use of external applications, as they are perceived to be poor at it relative to building stuff in house. And you can see where they are coming from: if you have total control of an application (a Client Relationship Management (CRM) System, for instance), you can hook it all completely to your billing systems, making sure one talks to the other at every level. This is seen as the nirvana, something you cannot achieve with applications you cannot control. This is misguided on two grounds. First, like all nirvanas, you never actually get there: there is not one firm I know that has actually succeeded in integrating all their systems with each other. Hang on, you say, it's just a matter of time: these things are complex beasts, and there's not always the money to do everything at once (in fact there is never the money to do everything at once). True, but the conclusion you must draw from this is that you will take longer to integrate your applications than the time those applications remain appropriate and best in class for your business to use. In other words, by the time you have connected everything up, everything connected is obsolete. As a consequence, whilst the outside world is brimming with newer, more capable, less expensive technology tools, the tradition business must ignore them in a dogged pursuit of gold-plating their vision of yesterday's challenges? Who benefits? Certainly not those responsible for generating the revenue.

This brings me onto the second reason why blanket integration is wrong-headed (and unachievable). The desire to achieve this is, in part, due to a belief in the need to "industrialise" service businesses as our forebears did with factory production. Underlying this is the drive to imbue the "system" with as much knowledge as possible, leaving the firm less dependent on the efforts of skilled staff – in short make machines act like people, and people like machines. The results are undeniably bad (as I discussed in the first part of this book) with clients and employees scurrying round the outside of monstrous, unyielding blocks of grey software, both waiting in line for an audience with The Great One at one entry point, only to be told to scurry round to another one afterwards and wait again for the next process. The whole thing smacks of some Kafka-esque bureaucracy you might easily have found in a 1950's fascist dictatorship. The fundamental point is that machines are good at being machines (they do the same thing every time, they don't have aspirations, they don't gossip near the watercooler) and people work best as people (they can make decisions based on an infinite (and changing) set of variables, they build trust with other people, they can fix things with an ingenuity unknown to machines). People in business tend to work in three ways: in relationships with clients and suppliers, in core product creation, or in the tracking of money. Hey presto, that corresponds to the Datastore architecture proposed above. Thus integration is only really important within each Datastore, something that can (and is) easily catered for by external applications. Thus you are left with a different, less cynical view of a service business: one where the flexible input of human beings is celebrated and encouraged, whilst that unique pool of skill and judgement (for that is what you will create) is aided by systems that give their judgement some scalable *velocity*. Think of it as sculpture with chainsaws. Built in such a way, each "pot" vibrates independently to the rhythm of their own requirements; new CRM systems that allow for richer interaction with clients can be brought in, new adjuncts and upgrades to product systems can be accommodated and new modules bolted on to cope with yet another change to taxation rules can quickly be installed without fear of upsetting the other parts of the business.

Of course, every firm's detailed processes within each Datastore will be unique, so it is impossible to go through every conceivable example here. There are, however, some important considerations to keep in mind as our intrepid entrepreneurs attempt to map out what they do. The first and most important thing they have to do is to keep the aim uppermost in their thoughts. This sounds simple, but is actually quite difficult to do, and very rarely accomplished in any business. Let's use one example to illustrate my point when the new firm is considering something close to the heart of many businesses: mobile email. To do it right, they should not think "blackberry", rather they should be thinking "mobile messaging". This will enable them to conceive of the need in its generic form, rather than a particular solution. Why? Surely they are one and the same? Well, no actually. For one thing, thinking of the aim rather than the solution gives them crystal clarity as to whether they really need to pay for what blackberry offers (and, of course, they might), and it will allow them to swap the solutions as their requirements change (or the technology lurches forward) – this generation is wedded to email, the next very much to instant messaging. Relying on their solution provider to interpret their messaging needs and respond as they change with the new firm's interests at heart is to harbour a touching faith in the preparedness of their suppliers to behave with other-worldly altruism.

Outputs and Constituencies

Now that the new firm has defined (at the lowest level of granularity) what it needs to do and what information it needs to do it with, it's time for our intrepid entrepreneurs to consider the exact nature of their output, and who needs to consume that output. To connect this to my earlier passage on architecture, this is the process by which the Reporting Layer is initially configured. In the same way as our new team needed to avoid the pitfalls of received wisdom when charting their processes, so they need to avoid hackneyed thinking when considering the outputs. Typically, the common misconception is to define output as *reports*. Of course, one form of an output could be a document (which is what most people mean when they say "report"), but it might not be. Just as we wanted to get to the lowest level of detail when charting the input and process map, so they should with output, which means understanding the things that make up the information contained in the report.

Indeed, getting to the bits that might sit inside the closed report is vital. First, it may be that their consumer (whether internal or external) is simply taking the firm's report and extracting a targeted subset of information contained in the report. Not only is the firm going through unnecessary cost in combining data that is best transmitted separately, but their consumer is also faced with an extra task of ripping the report open to get at what they really want. By making everything available at the lowest level and in combinations chosen by the consumer, the firm can save time and money by avoiding an extra collation step themselves and will win serious brownie points with their consumers as they offer a service attuned to their needs - the holy grail of mass-customisation.

Of course, to a control freak this smacks of suicidal frankness. Surely the job of client reporting (if that is what we are talking about here) is all about spinning the message, presenting the facts in such as way as to bathe the firm in as wonderful a light as possible? Letting the client chose their own subset of information in the way suggested here represents an unacceptable loss of control. This is muddled and self-defeating thinking. In the old world of controlled client reporting, the clients were never controlled, *but frustrated:* they knew that they were being spun to, but could do nothing about it, except never give that firm the benefit of the doubt. Everyone makes mistakes, but the firm who attempts to spin them will suffer far more than the firm who is honest about it. Remember that a firm's market exists in the minds of its clients and potential clients: what they want and how the firm can help them get it in the future. Being "spun to" destroys the trust necessary to allow your potential clients to link their needs with your solutions if they have a choice. (You may not be in a business that reports much to your clients, of course, but the same arguments apply to "clients" of your output who are in another department of your firm).

As should be obvious by now, there should be no systematic distinction between internal and external users of the firm's output. Perhaps a helpful analogy is to think of the Reporting Layer as a kind of virtual supermarket. Information is laid out on shelves, clearly marked for consumption. A variety of people can enter this super-market, from the smallest client wanting a single piece of information to the CEO, whose purview extends across the store. This image raises all kinds of security questions in people's minds - if everybody accesses the same system to get their information, what is stopping Mrs Miggins seeing the confidential Board Papers on the next hostile acquisition? The answer lies in ensuring that the external application(s) you are using to power the Reporting Layer possess a security model sophisticated and robust enough to capture and manage needs of each user accord-ing to their entitlement to the information (and there are plenty of them around), and that you have a business process robust enough to ensure that each user is set up correctly. For those who are interested, this security architecture is called the "Jericho Model", where entitle-ment is set at the data level, not the application or network level (tearing down the walls, geddit?).

It is at this stage that you might question the need for such an "open" model, given the risks. This would be wrong as we have seen, because to discriminate would be to pass up the opportunity to build your system around the "Real Network" that links everyone connected with the business. Second, to split your systems is to double the price. So which risk are you going to take on, that of inadvertent disclosure or bloated P&L?

The exact configuration of the Reporting Layer will, of course, be dependent on the exact needs of each business (which will change over time). However, some principles to guide our intrepid new firm:

Being a tool to allow their clients access to their information (and also a vital element of the firm's plan to continue operating in the event of a disaster) it is important that the application(s) they select to render this information can operate as independently as possible from the platforms their users will employ to gain access to the information. The obvious answer here is that they should use a browser-based application, of course, but beware some "gotchas": As the complexity of the information they wish to show increases (and the greater the user interactivity they desire), so does the need to think beyond the browser to other technologies to give the end user a "desktop experience". I will talk about this in more detail in the techie section that follows this one, but suffice to say that there are right and wrong answers on this one.

The Reporting Layer is a bit like an iceberg: most of the important stuff is below the waterline. It's the ability to organise all their various data items into some sense that will allow for reporting that is genuinely insightful. As I mentioned when I introduced the concept of the Reporting Layer, the Firm needs to go through a process of building a series of "reference tags" for the key items of data in all three Datastores, so that each item is understood in relation to any other item. Presumptuously, this is a bit like a home-spun (and rather basic) version of the great Tim Berners Lee's concept of the "Semantic Web" where he argues for the next phase of web development to be around the ability of web agents not only to render third party content on the page (the browsers of today) but also to *read and understand the content,* so that (for instance), the browser would understand that a group of words on Tesco's website is in fact a list of items for sale. For that to work across the web requires huge thought, global agreement on commons forms of data tagging and possibly a couple more generations of wowzer disruptive technology, so I'll leave it to Tim to save the world for a second time. However, to do a basic version for our new firm is a far more do-able thing: let's call it *the Semantic Company.* In completing their Virtual Audit, our firm is well on the way to charting all the important nodal points of their business and the nature of the information required by different consumers of their output. As we have discovered, all businesses are really the same: they do stuff for clients for a fee. Thus the single thread tying all three Datastores to each other is the client: where they live, what the firm does for them, who looks after them at the firm, how much the firm charged them last time, when the next bill for the client will be despatched, what we said to the client at the last meeting etc. You get the message. Thus, through the "client", all things the firm does can be understood in relation to each other, and combined in all sorts of ways. In the next section, I'll go into more detail as to how to do this using the latest technology. (Of course, I have made no mention of processes within a firm that do not include the client, such as HR. Building the semantic layer around the client is a good way of spotting those things that do not fit easily into this model. These things should be got rid of, or at least minimised).

Lastly, our new firm should not pass up the opportunity of using the Reporting Layer to *brand the provision of information.* Of course, at its most simplistic this means that its reporting output needs to have the same look and feel no matter what form the output takes: thus an online view of a client's data should be immediately recognisable as having come from the same style family as a printed report that they might receive. All obvious stuff, and well understood, I think. However, what is less obvious is the opportunity to brand the *way* information is published that reflects the firm's unique values and reinforces the firm's USP. Here is an example from my industry, the investment management business, and specifically Majedie Asset Management. Our USP was (and is) the skilful way we believed we picked the individual shares that formed part of our clients' portfolios, allied with a great deal of honesty and openness in showing the clients the effects of our decisions: which shares we had got right, and which we had got wrong (called "attribution", in the trade). In this way we could inculcate a sense of reassurance for our clients, even as (inevitably) we did not get everything right.

In building the Reporting Layer, we realised that the bit about attribution would be vital: not only to give visibility to an area that we kept telling clients was one of the most important, but to do so in a way that would reinforce our claims to be transparent, honest and helpful (and exhibit enough confidence in ourselves by contemplating "lifting our skirts" in this way). The way attribution had traditionally been displayed was within a table, with a list of the biggest share winners and losers in clients' portfolios on the left, showing on each row that share's weighting in the portfolio relative to the index weighting of that share, and the effect on the total portfolio return (positive or negative) of holding that share over a particular period. All very samey across the industry. Instead, we hit upon the idea of showing the same information but graphically: each share represented a cross on a graph whose axes were relative weighting and return effect. As each of the values could be negative, the graph was like a cross with four quandrants: top right for stuff we held in greater concentration than the index that had done well (which had benefited performance), top left for stuff that we had less than the index (or none at all) which had done badly so also beneficial, bottom right for stuff we held more of than the index which had done badly (so had hurt performance) and stuff on the bottom left that we didn't own much of (or none at all) which had done well, again a boo-boo. Not only did it give us and our clients a more helpful graphical view on such data, the system allowed clients to pick the period to do the analysis, often meaning that they would ask questions of us about reports that we as employees had not seen ourselves: the old fashioned control freaks would throw their hands up at this point, fretting over how that would "make us look". The clients on the other hand seemed very reassured by our behaviour: if we had something to hide or lacking in confidence in our ability to outperform, would we give them unfettered access to the data? Thus the tool had performed two important business tasks, to provide clear, unique information about a critical process to all interested parties, and to reinforce our claim to be open and honest.

So, our new firm has completed its Virtual Audit, and is therefore now thoroughly acquainted with its information requirements. It's now time for the rubber to hit the road, time to acquire some stuff to manage these requirements. I'll deal both with the initial procurement of a new system, and also with situations where modifications/links should be constructed to existing systems.

How Systems Work

You'll be pleased to hear that I am not going to go through in gory detail how every conceivable system might work (I define "system" as a collection of computing resources delivering the firm's information, or a given subset of it): it would be beside the point for our intrepid entrepreneurs, and quickly very out of date. What I will aim to do below is to introduce the very general technology concepts behind all systems, highlighting the different options and their pros and cons. Remember that the trick for our entrepreneurs when faced with the challenge of systems assembly is to keep their focus on their requirements, not on the vagaries of different potential solutions. However, when talking through the potential solutions with IT salesmen, it is important to understand what they are talking about (which is more than some of those salesmen are capable of).

What should become apparent is that, whilst technology vendors would have you believe that their product is the only possible solution to your problem, the real issue is to choose between a myriad of different ways to address your needs, with no single right answer: that's why building such systems can be so difficult for people usually charged with the task: senior computer people.

Temperamentally attached to the binary logic of the motherboard, making design calls on a system based on qualitative criteria to choose between many right answers is an anathema. So, great efforts are expended to "harden" the criteria: exhaustively transparent, structured beauty parades for software solutions are run, qualitative considerations are mangled into "score sheets" all designed to allow a single right answer to drop out. Except that the eventual answer was not one of the original right answers, not least because the system is now designed for the score sheet, not (the ever-shifting) reality. Still, the process allows IT to point to a "best in class procurement system" if anyone subsequently complains of any shortcomings.

Bear in mind that your "system" can (and of course should be) virtual: it is a description of the assets used in the handling of your firm's information, not simply an inventory of the computers (and their software) your company has on its balance sheet. Note also that the "assets" in your system deployed to handle your information need not even be physically connected to each other, except in the sense that they be viewed through the same employee (or client) browser. Our entrepreneurs have remembered enough of their training to be thinking of three hubs to design around: The firm's wider context (Relationship Datastore), management of key processes (Operational Datastore), and management of the accounts (Financial Datastore), all with the Reporting Layer on top. The word "hub" is important, as it tells our new firm that each third of this system is an independent entity, spinning in its own orbit with its own trajectory. Do not fall for the siren voices of single solutions or blanket integration: it will never satisfy enough of the needs of the specialists in each area (leading to a spreadsheet revolt) and will be torn apart by shifting reality. However, just because they spin in their own orbits does not mean that they should not relate to each other: as we have seen, the thread through all of them is the client. Attention should be paid to the ability of any potential software solution to produce output necessary in another part of the business or by external parties. Because they have done their Virtual Audit, our entrepreneurs are crystal clear as to exactly what outputs are required. And so onto the nitty-gritty of software solutions. In this section, my aim is to equip business users with starting grasp of some of the language used by technologists to describe their systems in order that, through iterative questioning, they can get a conceptual feel for *how the software is designed to work*. Why is that important? Surely it is sufficient to understand what the salesman says are the benefits of their system, and how they might solve the firm's problems? This is where it all usually goes wrong in the business/IT conversation (whether the "IT" is an external vendor or an internal department). Thus IT will spend enormous amounts of time trying to understand the business, but the business will avoid getting too close to the software for fear of catching some contagious disease, as if an understanding of technology is not compatible with a balanced approach to life. This is strange and hugely value-destructive. It's strange because technology plays such a central part of every business person's life – far more than the accounts, which are done by accountants and are the subject of much business school lust. Accounts merely keep the score, whereas technology (and information management in general) can *change* the score. It's value-destructive because it's a whole lot easier for business people to gain a sound conceptual grasp of technology that it is for IT outsiders to understand how a business works. It typically takes a professional business person no more than 15 minutes to understand how a system works. If it takes more than that, then either that business person isn't listening, or the vendor rep doesn't understand it either. Once that system insight is gained, it is then relatively easy to consider if it works for the business.

This is turning a generation of accepted practice on its head. In this brave new world, it is the business person who is in charge of any procurement initiative, leaving the technologists to carry out "closed" commands: please link this field with that one in a different system etc. There is no "capture the business requirements" phase that has proved so lucrative for software vendors in the past. Besides it being a lot easier to understand a new technology solution at the architectural level than it is to get to grips with a business (and a lot cheaper and faster), there are another couple of big advantages. First, you can spot business problems that would be addressed by a particular piece of software that the vendor itself may not be aware of. Second, in addition to unexpected portability, there is the issue of suitability: not trying to get the software to do something it was not fundamentally designed to do. And so onto the tech stuff.....

How to Structure Your Systems: Clients and Servers

These terms are bandied around with great frequency in technical circles, and these terms sit at the heart of any proposed information architecture. When they talk about the client, they don't mean *your* client, but a piece of code that sits with the end computer (more on types of client in the section below) and consumes the information served up by the server. To give you an example in everyday business life, a fairly commonplace client is Microsoft Outlook, receiving updates from another familiar piece of business computing, a Microsoft Exchange server. It is the server that does the heavy lifting gathering all the email from other servers that has been transmitted from around the world. Once received, it is forwarded to all relevant inboxes (Outlook) in the company. In this case, think of the mail client as your in tray, and the server the mail room. Of course such clients do not have to be run by computers: the growth of mobile email (or "push" email) is largely due to the maturing of a capable mail client for the mobile phone (from such providers as RIM (Blackberry) and Microsoft) and corresponding enhancements to servers to allow them to keep relatively secure links over the airwaves to such clients. The term "Client Server" is often used to describe the period in systems architecture when the prevailing use of mainframes and dumb terminals (think black screen with green lettering) gave way to a more distributed balance of computing resource, pushing many of the capabilities of the mainframe to the downstream computers, prompting an explosion of productivity: no longer was the sole processing resource located in one place, but split to a myriad of smaller PCs, all capable of operating (and thinking) independently through the use of "smart clients": fed with raw data from the centre, but equipped to enrich that data in ways not obvious to those cocooned from the rough and tumble of the trenches at mainframe headquarters. This is the era of Bill Gates: his decision to licence Microsoft's Windows operating system to different hardware manufacturers allowed for the development of de facto standards in business software, so driving benefits of scale and the chance to equip a large number of processors in a firm with standardised, (relatively) cheap means of writing stuff that others in the firm could understand (compatible file formats, in other words). And, as the Microsoft revolution rolled on, those benefits of standardisation began to seep across the inter-firm divide, allowing files to be swapped across the internet between companies, so turbo charging the business dialogue. Whereas before "by return" meant within a week for the exchange of letters, now to take more than a day to respond to an client email request with a new spreadsheet is considered tardy. Wonderful. Not only did the client server revolution "democratise" the ability to generate business output, it allowed for that output to be sent swiftly to its destination deep inside another firm and bypass the lumbering bureaucracy of the centralised post room and mail trolley. Or did it? Not really. For post room, read Microsoft Exchange Server, for mail trolley read the Local Area Network (LAN). Whilst the first stage of the client server revolution managed to speed things up considerably, it merely took the modus operandi of the recent past and mapped it to software: even the structure of the operating systems, with their "files" and "folders" smacks of the method of rendering information and method of storing it respectively. For all the whizzy code being deployed, it all still comes down to a fancy pencil case (an office suite of applications) and a fast horse (email).

Of course, in some instances it remains as appropriate to publish information encapsulated within files and held within folders and squirt them to someone else's letterbox as it ever was. Legal documentation, matters of policy etc should all be rendered in this way, as they are "controlled information" - if they were spoken, it would be in the form of a monologue, a set speech. Thus our modern business needs to have the standard "clients" used to create documents that are so familiar to traditional businesses: word processors, spreadsheet and presentation authors etc.

However, such "closed" forms of communication form only part of the range of business communication, both within a business and outside. For every instance of formal speech there are many more of dialogue, where the conversations revolve around relatively few questions: what do you want? Where are we with this? What can you tell us? In these circumstances, using the tools of monologue to render the dialogue is wrong (but astonishingly common). In this sense, the tools we currently use make sense to the transmitter (or, in this case, the supplier) of information. However, they make less sense to the receiver (or consumer) of the data. Bundling everything together in a closed document might make sense for the supplier of information, but not for the consumer who only wants what is relevant to them.

To illustrate this, consider it in the context of a railway station where there is a crowd of travellers waiting for information about trains to their chosen destination. This railway company has decided to employ a "state of the art" public address system to broadcast departure information for all destinations every 15 minutes, bang on time. This may be very efficient for the station master, as he gets great economies of scale: but for the traveller this is murderously frustrating, especially if you live in Yeovil and have to wait to the end of the announcement (doubly frustrating if the train itself leaves halfway through the announcement). Triply frustrating for those living in Ambleside and who came into the announcement halfway through – they will have to wait to the next scheduled announcement. Of course this does not happen in real life, as train companies have learn to lay their information out as an "open book" allowing consumers to "graze" on the bits they want.

This, however, is a rare exception, as most companies are stuck at the document stage. Sure they understand the need to be relevant to their clients, but they choose to solve this in a mangled way using hugely expensive customising engines to produce individual closed documents (a mail merge on steroids). They do this for a number of reasons. First, most people are still stuck with the inability to distinguish between a document and the information contained within it (see Part One above), and second they are frightened of losing the editorial control of what and how the clients see their data. What they should be doing is developing a common platform capable of being viewed by all (internal and external) tied to a simple security model that governs entitlement to data: If you are internal, you can see all that firm's (or departments) output: if you are an external client, you can only see the output for you.

So it follows that, just as there are different types of inter-actions so there should be different types of clients and servers to support them. This is most true of the kit that our firm will use in the Reporting Layer, let's start there. It is also right to start from the "front" before moving to the "back" (to the Operational and Financial Datastores, particularly), as this ensures our entrepreneurs are demand, rather than supply led. As with all systems procurement, it is important to start with those requirements that are the most difficult to deliver and those that are of the highest priority. Interlay those two "stretch" criteria on top of each other and they quickly know those boxes they simply have to tick. In the case of the Reporting Layer, the most important box to tick is almost always *Ubiquity* - how to make sure information can be accessed anywhere, with almost any type of computer. Being demand led, our people settle on the challenge what client to use.

Very quickly it will become obvious that a single piece of technology may not fit the bill: for clients, the ability to see their information without having to download a particular bit of software is really important, and argues for the requirement that information must be accessible via a webpage (or "thin client" in the jargon, as there is little or no local footprint on the machine viewing the data). However, for internal staff handling huge quantities of data, a more capable application might be in order that has more of the code installed with the end user ("thick client"). In addition, "thin clients" require the presence of a data connection to display anything, whereas a "thick" alternative can usually work "offline", making such an application useful to employees on the move.

The "thin/thick" thing used to be a simple binary choice: you either used a simple web page which could be called from any processor with a connection, but whose user experience was slow and cludgy, or downloaded a massive application that threw the data around like professional wrestler, but whose system requirements where fussy and depended on constant ego-strokes from an expensive IT department. However, that has now changed, with a whole bundle of "intermediate" technologies that combine some of the best of both worlds: browser-based systems that store ("cache") certain subsets of data offline, "thicker" clients that are not so choosy about the operating system they find themselves mounted on, and browsers that behave almost as cleverly as their thick clients ("web 2.0 technologies"). The key at this stage (and in most stages) is not to get suckered down some proprietary path, in the pocket of some vendor and sticking out like a sore thumb to your customers, who need to do something special and additional to be able to connect to you. In this space it means starting with the lightest "footprint" our firm can get away with on its clients' computers, ideally by aping the delivery mechanism used by the biggest web-based applications like Google: at the moment that would be via simple web pages with JavaScript enabled, utilising small and unobtrusive streams of stuff to flow between the server and the webpage without having to refresh the entire web page when you want to tweak something on it. That's how you can resize Google maps on the fly, and drag and drop emails in yahoo's webmail system.

Another advantage of using popular technology for the Reporting Layer (or any other part of the architecture, for that matter) is that those with the right skill set will be relatively plentiful, and the technology well tested. Remember, having an innovative service does not mean having to live on the "bleeding edge" of technology: it means delivering new information and new insight. Doing so with tried and tested technology lessens the risks of the project and probably lowers the cost as the skills necessary will be competitively priced. To give you an example from my own business, we needed to build an enhanced reporting tool from an existing supplier of risk information about our portfolios: the system spat out three excel spreadsheets ("flat files" in the jargon) and we wanted to combine them automatically into one. The application provider was asked to quote for the code necessary to do this, and they said it would cost $14,000, including $6,000 for "project management" to ensure this staggeringly complex piece of software engineering could be kept on track. We then went to www.getacoder.com, a reverse auction site where technologists globally can pitch for business. Our winner quoted $123, and he did the job flawlessly.

There will be many in the IT community who will be shocked by such behaviour. Where was the quality control? Who is going to support the application going forward? Let's look at all of those things in turn. The first point, wondering whether it works or not is simple. It either does or it doesn't. You don't pay until you've tested the solution, and it's clear whether it does the job. And even if you manage to part with your money without securing a positive outcome you have wasted the equivalent of paying for some external consultant's time for 30 minutes. The secret is not to follow the same procurement route for a full CRM system, but that's just common sense. Second, the question of support. It is true that full-time support for certain core parts of your system in use by the firm every day should be looked over by system experts – that's why the Software as a Service offer is so compelling. However, for many other parts of the system that are only periodically used (this report was needed for client reports once every three months) there is no need to pay an expensive premium because A) the code is relatively straightforward and B) it is written in one of the most common languages, Visual Basic. Don't change things around it, and it won't fall down. Because an externalised system is well dispersed and not linked too heavily to each other, the risk of contagion (one system change bringing down other parts of the system) is all but eliminated.

In addition to ensuring that our firm becomes a technology "chameleon" and bends to the prevailing technology winds when considering how best to do the job, there is another principle that applies to all technology procurement: follow the "honey pot". There are some technologies that become the hubs around which many independent developers will buzz: two that spring to mind at the moment are Microsoft Sharepoint (essentially an intranet in a box) and Salesforce.com (a Software –as –a Service vendor of relationship tracking software – and much more besides). Both pieces of software benefit from the virtuous circle that comes from their popularity – the more ubiquitous they are, the more third party vendors will write systems that complement and extend their functionality, and so the more popular they become. It is vital that our new firm picks software for its hubs that fit this particular bill. Not only will they be able to fit other pieces of the jigsaw that have already done the heavy lifting of integration with the core systems, our entrepreneurs stand much more chance of persuading a software company whose application they like to bear the costs of integration if they can persuade them that it will enhance the software's saleability to other clients.

How to Structure Your Systems: Getting your Data Ducks in a Row

Having dealt with the uppermost layer of the new firm's architecture, I am now going to leapfrog the bits in the middle (the applications that the firm uses to do their stuff, and the "glue" to bring the important bits of the information together) and dive down into the depths of the architecture, where the information is stored. Why do it in this order? First, to do the data before considering the applications that might sit on top is to recognise that the former is vastly more important than the latter, even if it is rarely visible to the naked eye.

It will come as no surprise to you that our intrepid entrepreneurs should consider this problem (like almost all the other ones) *virtually*. That is to say that in drawing up the plans for the data layer, the firm should not make the mistake of rushing out to procure great servers and buy lots of database licences in anticipation of establishing a physical database (or even to dash off and hire a hosting company to do the same thing). In the same way that the Virtual Audit helped define the scope for the Reporting

Layer (types of output and constituency), so it will be key to the data plan. In establishing exactly what the firm's inputs need to be, they have already gone most of the way to understanding the outline of the data storage plan. The *virtual* bit comes in when the firm starts to assess how they might actually put the rubber on the road and rent some stuff. Before they can really get going, our team needs a few simple pointers about this area.

In the same way that they did for the Reporting Layer, our team must use a database technology that is *popular*. Because their virtual database will in practise be spread among many physical databases it is not necessary to have a singular database technology (that would cut down the list of possible business applications, as many of the databases used will come integrated with them), but that they are all in fairly common usage in the technology world. The biggest decision our team will have to make is whether they do go with some sort of their own repository (run for them by a hosting company, naturally) or rely on the cluster of databases that sit under the applications they choose. There is no hard and fast rule to this, and will depend on the demands of the application layer above, particularly the tool that gathers the reference pieces of data for meaningful combinations in the Reporting Layer: can the tool gather them all from the databases serving the team's business applications, or does it need some sort of a buffer, a "data departure lounge"?

Regardless of all that, the really important point is that, for the data plan to work, there must be a careful survey done in the Virtual Audit, and a clear idea of where the primary version of that data is in the architecture. A good example is the concept of an "address". Being something associated with the client, it is something that will most probably sit in all three Datastores, Relationship, Operational and Financial. However, one of the Datastores should have clear ownership of it, and the other two should hold reference copies. Thus when a client writes in with a change of address it should be reflected in the Relationship Datastore, and the changes promulgated to the Operational and Financial Datastores. Thus service visits by the Maintenance Department will go to their new address, and bills will hit their target. Our team shouldn't worry too much at this stage as to how to engineer the promulgation, it is enough to establish a firm, unique home in a database whose technology is reasonably modern and accessible.

And now onto the bit that does actually involve business people interacting directly with technology – at last I hear you say. There is a reason that this piece comes right at the end of the passage on setting up your own information system - because the choice of application should actually be postponed until you have all the other bits done. You wouldn't attempt to build walls and a roof before you have completed the foundations, would you? By establishing the nature of your own Information Map – its key constituents, its junctures, its associations and its audience – many of the answers for the information layer will be obvious. Some examples: if you establish that much of the work in a particular process occurs outside the company boundaries, then an application's architecture is more important than its functionality – it needs to be web-based, even if that offers a less rich environment to the user. If however, a key process is complicated, of high intensity but managed by only a relatively small number of internal staff, then an application that installs onto a local PC is probably wise, given that functionality is more important than ubiquity. At this stage, some people might be getting confused. Surely this is all about "cloud computing" the use of web based applications? Not necessarily. It is perfectly possible to deploy "thicker" applications into an enterprise and still maintain that business' direct interaction with it (examples include deploying Microsoft Outlook as the front end to an outsourced Exchange server) without the need for expensive support. The key is that all these external applications are *balanced*: that is to say, they can survive on their own two feet. This is in contrast to the Local Area Networked world, where much of the technology is deployed like the poles of a wigwam: remove one and watch the rest of it wobble. Thus the *type* of application is less important than how the business can interact with it. If it needs someone to manage it for you (and only your deployment), don't buy it.

OK, so that's my best stab at equipping you with the right thoughts on how you would approach this challenge from a clean sheet of paper. However, I am well aware that most people will not be doing that, but thinking: "it's all very well, but it wouldn't work in my environment where legacy technology, people and processes are well embedded". This next section deals with this eventuality.

I will start with a confession: I said at the start of this book that this method of working had been well-tested for seven years at Majedie Asset Management. Up to this point, that statement holds true. Every thought jotted thus far has been how we did it. However, this next section is different: to my knowledge, this has not been attempted before anywhere.

Before you stop there and put the book down, it is worth noting that I have absolutely no doubt that such a transformation is necessary and possible. Necessary because it really behoves each business to be as efficient as it can be, not least for competitive reasons. It is possible because you have the same raw material as for the clean sheet example: business people and modern, balanced applications. So instead of blue sky thinking by the business founders as to what the ideal structure might be, there needs to be a roadmap produced of where an existing business is now and how it needs to get to a better place (cynics of this book might call it a *project*). The two key principles of this book to bear in mind at this stage are: the separation of the management of a firm's information from its business structure, and that only *balanced applications* should be considered for the future – another way of putting it is that business people need to be able to work the systems without recourse to IT to "support" them.

So, onto the first principle. Because all legacy businesses have IT staff sprinkled within them (either salaried or on outsourced contracts), any initial moves to change the information structure will involve pretty wholesale changes to the IT department. In most businesses, the IT department has made strenuous efforts to get "aligned with the business" and so, with a few exceptions, will mirror the structure of the firm. This is wholly counter-productive, and needs to be changed so that it is aligned around the structure of the firm's *information*. To do this properly you need to keep in mind the *Virtual Audit* you have done to establish what the firm's input, key process, output and audience requirements are. By now you will have understood how important that audit process is, and how vital it is that it is done by knowledgeable business people, not IT. To do otherwise would have produced something neatly cut by business unit, hugely duplicatory and immobile. Business ownership of the Virtual Audit, conducted using the structure of the three Datastores will ensure that common solutions can be found in the Relationship and Financial buckets, and even the Operational Datastore will be less fragmented than it might be as business people can play the "type of" game much more effectively than IT staff.

Once the Information Map has been created, it then becomes possible to orientate some of your existing IT staff to each nodal point on it. Once there, their job is very different to the one they did before: In legacy organisations, IT staff either represented an application (or core technology) and managed its interaction with departments, or represented a department and managed its interaction with applications (and championed the department in spending rounds to buy or build applications to support a specific departmental need). In the new world, our IT bod will be asked to manage a specific information need for the whole business: this will entail understanding how each part of the business operates, and helping one part of the business learn from another.

Of course, all this changes little in the IT engine room: whilst you might have cracked the task of separating your information management from the business structure, your technology deployed to support it is still stubbornly stuck in the twentieth century - expensively dependent on direct support, immobile and duplicatory. At least now you can see the duplication: having done the Virtual Audit and boiled down the information needs of each part of your business and having individuals singularly in charge of fulfilling those requirements, the myriad of different applications supplying essentially the same thing will be obvious, as will the excess cost. Now comes the time to start swapping the expensive internal mess with cheaper balanced applications that the business can configure and run itself. It is at this stage that most legacy opposition is encountered: surely we can't expect to run our sophisticated, unique business with some simple standardised tools from the web? Actually, it is your people that are sophisticated and unique. The technology tools may be standard, but the way they use them will not.

To understand how this can be true, you should conduct the following experiment: within your business, find a typical department and within that outfit identify the super user (there's always one person who knows how it all works). Then take that super user into a room with nothing but a computer and an internet connection, and ask them to use the search engine and find free web-based applications (or downloads) that he/she could use to support their department's operations in the event that none of the current technology was available. This exercise will show you that most of the department's needs can be catered for by nothing but free applications found on the web, and those requirements that are not immediately fulfilled can be changed to fit the new environment with surprisingly little loss of capability.

What that exercise is designed to achieve is not to prove that you can run your business using Google spreadsheets and other free applications on the web, but that the real value of your business is with your people, not your systems. The exercise has also started to show your best business people how to procure technology: find out what it has to offer, and work out how to use it best, changing business processes as necessary to take advantage of what the applications have to offer. You will also have taken the first step in a) putting humans at the centre of your information network, displacing the "system" and b) identifying those people best suited to get involved in the information management plan for the future.

So, you have redeployed some of your IT staff and introduced your business to the new form of procurement, where do you do from there?

You start the procurement process in earnest, using teams of new redeployed IT staff and the business super users to pick the right solutions, retiring waves of your legacy infrastructure as you do so. As you progress, the hoped for cost savings will be initially modest. Much of IT's legacy will be needed for as long as a single department needs it, leading to delay. To ensure that the real cost of support is understood, the costs of those legacy services should be shouldered only by those departments still dependent on them. There will come a time, however, when the savings come thick and fast. For one thing, you will reach a point where the much-vaunted (and supremely costly) alternate location plans can be cast aside, as the globe becomes the alternate location.

So what does the modern enterprise look like when the transition is finished? Of course, there is no definable end point, as what I describe is more a different way of operating, rather than some capital-intensive plan (it is helped in that regard as most balanced applications come on a rental basis). I talked earlier in the book about organisations that can take back the control of their information that they hitherto outsourced to computer people, and that remains the best description of where you want to get to. However, I have made no mention of the ultimate fate of your IT people who were redeployed onto the management of your key nodal points: in a modern-day Night of the Long Knives, have they been turfed out in favour of newly-enthusiastic business managers? It depends on a number of things, but it's important to stress that the best of these IT employees have changed from *computer* to *information* people, so the change has been effected even if some people remain. I also talked about how this would represent the end of the network-centric view of IT, which it is: of course you will still be in need of some form of basic network to share your internet connections and printers. It might even stretch to providing some form of single sign on (one password covering multiple applications) for some of your systems. However, don't let the siren calls of this part of your system trick you into the retrograde step of allowing for structural internal IT resources. Your domain control function (i.e. the network administration) should be simple enough to be happily managed by a few business people, or, at a pinch, a few IT staff on an outsourced basis. Anything more demanding than that and you have the wrong strategy, a slippery slope towards the past.

So, there you have it. This book has been an attempt to demonstrate how important information is to a business, and how separate it is as a concept from technology. By separating out the two, a modern business can manage its information far better than before and at far lower costs. Some people will be disappointed that I did not lay out complete plan for converting to the new environment: as I have attempted to show, it is more about new thinking than some new process (indeed, the crux of the new thinking is to stop treating it like a process). When I see someone offering me a way of doing things that is better and cheaper, I always look for a catch: nothing is for free. The catch in this case is that businesses have to forget everything they have held dear for 20 years. The drive to construct a system with a built in competitive advantage, the desire to minimise dependence on key employees, the need to iron out uncertainty: these have to be replaced by a realisation that technology is just a tool, and it is in your people that you will find your comparative advantage, especially if they are allowed to work with the objective in mind, not the process.

Many people will read these words and give out a low whistle: that would be far too risky for our business – what a free-for-all. In this case, it is always instructive to work out what the "risk" is they are referring to. All too often it is the risk of losing control, which is not the same as the risk of a business underperforming. It is also the risk of being wrong, which nobody wants; in the days of plenty of money, it was always better for an employee to conceive a £100m budget and see it overrun by 5% than something costing £20m that then overruns by 25%. In these days of capital rationing, the £20m option is the only one on the table, and the Direct Computing method is the only way to deliver on this.

Most of the people concerned about the "risk" of this entrepreneurial approach are those who currently work within the existing technology/operational structures of a business, and they find the idea that they are not only redundant but a huge millstone is frankly insulting (I mean none of this personally). It all works reasonably well, by and large, they say: where it does not, it is understandable given the huge complexity of the challenge. However, when you ask those these people profess to serve, there is seething resignation. Seething because no matter how much you spend, nothing turns out to be as good as you had been led to believe (or even half as good, but certainly over budget). Resignation, because it seems there's no other way. This book gives the lie to this.

There will also be many people reading this book who frankly cannot make the link between how you might change the technology (as they see it) to transform the business. It's all a bit geeky and whilst this stuff all might get a little cheaper, it's not a game-changer. The point, of course, is that it's not about the technology; it's about how a business can transform their management of information, and, in so doing, elevate its status within the business. By so doing, the business takes on the internet form, processing at internet speed and with internet cost, allowing it to keep pace with its wider world. Allied with its newfound directional agility, such a business also waxes and wanes in a materialistically different way to those of the 20th Century. In other words, the Direct Computing model makes virtual the *structure* of a firm's information management effort, and with that aligns it in speed, agility and cost terms with the outside world, already in virtual form (of course information is virtual, as separate from departments, documents and technology as energy is from a piece of coal, as we have seen).

It's really just the logical extension of the drive to virtualise many of the *tools* used in information management that makes up the modern-day phenomenon called Cloud Computing: in this model, the software "bit" of a server can be separated from its hardware, allowing the virtual servers to swarm across banks of hardware, driving down costs and improving performance and agility (in the limited sense of being able to respond to a mouse click). All well and good, but it goes only so far: the savings that traditional businesses can glean from such architecture are relatively small, and the risks of change large (especially to an internal IT team). None of the business agility seen in the Direct Computing model can accrue, as the structure managing such virtualised architecture is depressingly physical: departmental heads, supported by their IT reps, "professional" procurement teams, due process etc. Cloud Computing therefore offers some nimbleness in the last mile of the information management journey: upstream, however (the other 99 miles), it's still the same as it was in 1900.

However, it is the advent of the Cloud that allows for the establishment of Direct Computing, in much the same way as the invention of cheap motor cars spawned the rise of the US suburb: it's not so important to understand what it *is* as to appreciate what it might *enable*.

Go for it.

Lightning Source UK Ltd.
Milton Keynes UK
UKOW05f1008290714

235948UK00001B/19/P